Buying Property in
FRANCE

Buying Property in
FRANCE

by Danny Lee

The author

Danny Lee practised as a solicitor until 1990. Since then he has written for national newspapers, such as *The Times* and the *Guardian*, on the law and an array of other subjects.

Text © 2005 Danny Lee

Lawpack Publishing Limited
76–89 Alscot Road
London SE1 3AW

www.lawpack.co.uk

All rights reserved
Printed in Great Britain

ISBN: 1 904053 74 2

The law is stated as at 1 July 2005

This Lawpack Pocket Guide may not be reproduced in whole or in part in any form without written permission from the publisher.

Exclusion of Liability and Disclaimer

While every effort has been made to ensure that this Lawpack Pocket Guide provides accurate and expert guidance, it is impossible to predict all the circumstances in which it may be used. Accordingly, neither the publisher, author, retailer nor any other suppliers shall be liable to any person or entity with respect to any loss or damage caused or alleged to be caused by the information contained in or omitted from this Lawpack Pocket Guide.

For convenience (and for no other reason), 'him', 'he' and 'his' have been used throughout and should be read to include 'her', 'she' and 'her'.

Contents

	Introduction	vii
1	**How to find the right property**	1
2	**The letter of the law**	11
3	**Finance facts**	21
4	**Checking your bricks and mortar**	27
5	**The renovation and build-your-own game**	33
6	**Business property and letting**	39
7	**Emigrating to France**	45
8	**What else should you consider?**	51
9	**Case studies**	57
	Glossary	63
	Appendix	69
	Index	81

 This Lawpack book is 'web enabled', meaning it is supported online with extra material. To access this, all you have to do is to register on the Lawpack website at:
www.lawpack.co.uk/propertyinfrance
entering the code below.

Registration code: **B4493140705**

Introduction

Many people dream of buying a home in France, tempted by the renowned food, wine, Gallic culture, gloriously varied countryside and unspoilt space of a nation more than twice the size of the UK. About 500,000 Britons have seen their fantasies come true and, if you want to follow them, you need to start doing your research, now.

'A growing number of people are falling foul of French law when they buy a home in France,' warns the UK solicitors' governing body, the Law Society. Rules and regulations set from Paris can often be very different from the property regime you are used to in the UK. Problems can, however, easily be avoided if you take the trouble to learn about, and perhaps even celebrate, the differences. If you do, you could soon be relaxing in your new home across the Channel, or rather 'La Manche'.

Listening to the stories of people who have already bought properties is one of the best ways to prepare yourself for the exciting and sometimes anxious journey ahead and this book includes the tales of several people who now own homes in France. They all have one thing in common. They all love their new properties.

With just 22 miles (35 kilometres) of sea separating it from Britain, France is one of the most popular destinations for international house hunters, whether they are looking for a holiday retreat or permanent home, and previously inaccessible areas are now within a short flight, thanks to low-cost airlines such as Ryanair, bmi and EasyJet. EU nationals or people from the European Economic Area who intend to make France their home, now also have the right to work there.

Buying Property in France

Rising property prices

The Dordogne generates the most interest, but the market is also pretty active in Normandy and Brittany in the north, and Languedoc-Roussillon and Provence in the south. Needless to say, all this activity has had the inevitable effect of fuelling property price rises around France. Property prices in France rose by 15.5 per cent in 2004, according to the Royal Institution of Chartered Surveyors. But house prices are still relatively low, compared with the UK, and low interest rates coupled with a stable economy add to the attraction of buying property in France.

Of course, rising property prices are all very good if you already own a property in France, but worrying if you are still looking to buy. You'll want to get your hands on a property as soon as you can, but you also do not want to end up making a mistake. You'll need to be cautious about how you spend your hard-earned money, particularly if you are tempted to seek a bargain by looking for unusual properties or homes in need of some tender, loving care.

Another result of the booming housing market is that a lot of non-French builders, developers and professionals are getting in on the act. This is great if you get involved with someone who knows what he is doing, but not so helpful if you end up with one of the less scrupulous operators.

Most of the trends in the French property market can work for you or against, but, to make sure you get the best possible deal, you will need to think about exactly why you want to buy a property in France, what you intend to do with it and where you want it to be. Just like the UK, prices vary hugely across the country and there are some areas where you would most definitely not want to own a property. In parts of Marseille, for example, there are racial tensions and many other cities have heavily industrialised zones, which would definitely not be conducive to either a relaxing holiday or a permanent home.

Introduction

Once you've worked out what you want, you will need to know a lot about the French legal system. Unlike the UK, for example, a preliminary contract (the *compromis de vente*) is often signed at an early stage, before the buyer has seen a lawyer. Many non-French people assume that this is an unimportant document, because it appears so early in the process. It is, in fact, binding on both the seller and the buyer, who can be forced by law to proceed with the transaction or face a costly legal action.

Keep your eyes open

You should not let your dream of an idyllic home abroad blind you to the seriousness of the commitment. To make sure that you don't make expensive and unnecessary mistakes, it is essential for you to find the right lawyer, or *notaire*. He will steer you through the process from the preliminary contract and payment of a deposit to the completion of the purchase, ensuring that your English legal affairs, such as Wills, are tied in with whatever you do abroad. Beware, for example, inheritance laws in France as they are not the same as in the UK.

Before doing anything about making your dream come true, though, you will need to deal with some very real, down-to-earth issues. At the top of this list should be your decision about your reason for buying the property. Is it simply a holiday home, or are you thinking of living in France permanently (in which case there may be immigration issues to consider as well as education rules, if you have young children)? If you want to set up, run or buy a business in France, there will be regulations governing how you go about it, particularly if it will be based in the property you are buying.

You should try to learn as much as you can about French culture before deciding to buy. Some areas are, for example, more conservative and less open to new residents or holiday homes than others. This can be particularly the case in

Buying Property in France

smaller villages in rural areas. Wherever you go, it can only help if you know something about the culture and language. This book includes a short guide or glossary to many of the legal and jargonistic words you will come across in the process of buying your property.

Money, money, money

Money should be next on your list. You will need to work out how much money you can afford or want to spend and whether you want to take a loan to cover any of the purchase price. You may need to consider mortgages, releasing equity in your UK property to buy in France, and the pros and cons of taking a French loan and borrowing in euros or taking a UK loan and borrowing in pounds.

A mortgage may not be what you want, but would an unsecured loan be better or, indeed, even possible? The property markets in France and the UK do not always do the same thing. In fact, at the moment, the UK market is fairly quiet, while the French market is booming. You will need to consider whether borrowing against a UK property will leave you exposed to the risk of negative equity if UK property prices fall. On the other hand, lending criteria in France are a lot stricter than in the UK, so, if you decide to go down the French finance route, you will need to think about whether you will be able to borrow enough money.

After finalising how much money you can spend, you will get to the fun, if sometimes exhausting, part of the process: finding the right property. To do this, there is a range of options: estate agents, agents who will, for a fee, look for a property for you, the internet and magazines, such as *Bonjour Magazine*, *Focus on France* or *France Magazine* and property fairs.

The one factor that is likely to affect your budget more than anything else is location. If you want somewhere warm, for example, the climate may affect where you buy. Are there certain regions that appeal to you more than others and what are their pros and cons? Are you attracted to tourist areas, for example the Dordogne, which may already be full of Brits and often more expensive, or do you want somewhere more authentically French? Do you want a rural, town, city, inland or coastal area? What should you consider if you want to let the property in the holiday rental market? What are the pros and cons of each option?

All these issues will affect the price of the property and determine what sort of home you will be able to buy, but if you want a holiday retreat, ease of access is likely to be a key factor. Do you want to be within a certain travelling time from the UK (in which case being near, but not too near, an airport may be important)? You will also need to be careful of being too reliant on flights that are pioneering access to new areas. If only a handful of budget airlines fly to a destination, they may stop their services or hike their prices if the route proves uneconomic.

A choice of old or new

After you decide on your location, you will need to consider the differences between new-build properties, buying off-plan and purchasing older, established properties. A lot of people find that it is cheaper in the long run to buy a wreck and renovate it slowly. This option also gives you the pleasure of putting your own stamp on the property, but you may need to be brave to manage French builders and other tradespeople. Whichever type of property you opt for, you will need to ensure that you know as much as possible about its condition. Even if you buy a wreck expecting to rebuild it, you will not want any nasty surprises that eat into your budget. Just like the UK, there may be numerous planning and building control issues to look out for, but, unlike the UK, many people buy properties without a survey.

Of course, you may decide to rent a property in France rather than buying there straight away or at all, but, needless to say, you will need to know about the law for that as well. And, knowing your rights and responsibilities will ensure that if and when you sell any home that you buy, you don't make any mistakes.

CHAPTER 1
How to find the right property

Property prices in France vary hugely, depending on the location, just the same as in most other countries. Then, within each location, there will be price variations dependent on the condition and size of the property. Many people know exactly where they want to buy before they start looking. It may, for example, be somewhere you have spent warmly-remembered holidays.

There are many questions to consider before you decide on a particular property. If you want somewhere warm, for example, the climate may affect where you buy. Are there certain regions that appeal to you more than others and what are their pros and cons? Are you attracted to tourist areas, for example the Dordogne, which may already be full of Brits, or do you want somewhere more authentically French? Do you want a rural, town, city, inland or coastal area? What should you consider if you want to let the property in the holiday rental market? Once you have decided on an area, do you want to buy a property to renovate or a home to move into straight away?

A word about local government

If you are not sure of where you want to buy, start off by learning about the names, positions and characteristics of the country's regions, departments and communes, based on the

Buying Property in France

country's constitutional settlement dating back to the 1789 revolution. These are the administrative bodies that deal with policy decisions for their parts of the country. This will also enable you to understand who is responsible for what, in a country that some people joke is obsessed by forms.

Region

France is divided into 22 'metropolitan' regions, including Corsica (plus four overseas: French Guiana, Guadeloupe, Martinique and Réunion). The regional council, whose members are elected for six years, deal mainly with planning, economic development and *lycées* (secondary schools for ages 15-17). A consultative assembly of businesses, and profession and trade union representatives advises on decisions.

Department

France's regions are subdivided into 96 departments. The *préfet* (prefect) represents the French state at departmental level. However, the general council, comprising councillors elected for a six-year term and a chairperson, is the department's decision-making body. The department is subdivided into arrondissements, thence into cantons (districts), each of which elects councillors to the council. There are 3,500 cantons throughout the country. The department deals with social services, health, roads and *collèges* (secondary schools for ages 11-15).

Commune

This is the bottom tier of French administration; there are approximately 37,000 communes (municipalities) throughout the country. Many of them have very small populations, many with fewer than 1,000 people. The municipal council, made up of councillors elected for six years, is the decision-making body. Its members elect a mayor. The council deals with local administration, the local economy and employment, and the management of local public buildings, such as primary schools. The mayor conducts weddings and he is also the registrar for births and deaths. He also has policing powers.

How to find the right property

The spice of life

Apart from the administrative side of life, knowing something about the different parts of France will help you enjoy the spice of its varied life. Different areas can be almost like different countries. The Mediterranean culture of the south is nothing like the city buzz of Paris, for example. When you know what each area is like and understand its benefits and problems (if there are any), it will clarify why some properties are cheaper than others and whether the lifestyle will be appropriate to you. This will enable you to spot potential properties more quickly when they arise.

If you want to buy a property mainly as an investment, you will need to consider where you are likely to get the best returns, through both value increases and rentals to visitors. You will, however, need to exercise caution. 'Spotting new French property hotspots can be a thrilling prospect, but the tried and trusted destinations still deliver the returns,' says Rob Campbell, principal of Totalplanet, internet overseas investment advisers. 'While ever greater numbers of us trawl the globe for the next big property hotspot, we should remember that some locations rarely lose their allure – as both a travel destination and a property goldmine.'

Campbell cites Cannes as an example. 'It hosts no less than a dozen festivals a year and so presents the perfect hunting ground for investors seeking reliable buy to let opportunities.' In many ways Cannes is unique, but it presents the perfect example of the sorts of issues that should be considered by anyone seeking to use his property as an investment. Property is not cheap, however. A one-bedroom apartment would cost at least €190,000, but demand for rental properties outstrips supply during festival periods, when this sort of property would be expected to produce between €1,500 and €2,900 a week rent. 'Agents estimate an annual rental yield for a typical

Buying Property in France

Average price of:	New* houses (euros)	Old houses (euros)	New flats (euros)	Old flats (euros)
FRANCE	**163,499**	**137,759**	**125,040**	**98,929**
Regions				
ALSACE	168,607	175,306	125,827	95,799
AQUITAINE	152,573	149,944	109,246	94,189
AUVERGNE	135,195	94,441	106,220	65,921
BASSE NORMANDIE	119,946	111,928	111,042	72,683
BOURGOGNE	132,045	103,924	110,018	77,831
BRETAGNE	153,641	132,280	113,413	85,148
CENTRE	135,929	114,545	105,538	74,474
CHAMPAGNE-ARDENNE	155,530	114,863	123,447	84,041
FRANCHE COMTE	130,761	117,098	108,673	73,703
HAUTE NORMANDIE	125,408	121,394	102,532	75,100
LANGUEDOC ROUSSILLON	149,281	165,696	113,328	79,586
LIMOUSIN	138,565	85,322	98,466	65,738
LORRAINE	150,131	120,235	105,939	80,849
MIDI PYRENEES	150,466	144,158	104,887	81,413

How to find the right property

	New* houses (euros)	Old houses (euros)	New flats (euros)	Old flats (euros)
NORD PAS-DE-CALAIS	146,153	111,208	110,546	91,471
PAYS DE LOIRE	140,981	127,314	116,831	92,182
PICARDIE	126,584	120,083	88,993	88,479
POITOU-CHARENTES	123,885	111,457	104,761	75,879
PROVENCE-COTE D'AZUR	249,981	286,060	153,670	126,926
RHONE-ALPES	211,435	188,752	140,922	107,992

* Less than 5 years old; otherwise, it is 'old'.

Land price information

	Average price (euros)	< 600 m²	600 – 1000 m²	1000 – 2500 m²	2500 – 5000 m²
FRANCE	42,313	34,321	42,814	44,311	43,673
Regions					
ALSACE	60,263	39,731	65,004	72,984	80,008
AQUITAINE	43,043	33,682	51,667	42,863	34,447
AUVERGNE	24,277	16,818	26,603	24,201	26,554
BASSE NORMANDIE	25,704	23,821	30,077	23,879	20,225
BOURGOGNE	25,875	22,150	30,484	24,462	22,692
BRETAGNE	34,202	32,273	34,187	35,931	33,200
CENTRE	29,099	22,494	34,978	27,750	24,641
CHAMPAGNE ARDENNE	32,475	32,052	36,518	29,662	27,341
FRANCHE COMTE	29,666	12,004	32,489	29,681	30,487
HAUTE NORMANDIE	29,107	24,104	33,601	28,180	26,873
LANGUEDOC ROUSSILLON	72,929	59,991	71,315	87,526	72,134
LIMOUSIN	21,181	16,875	25,903	20,389	18,783
LORRAINE	33,531	29,399	39,672	28,914	27,908
MIDI PYRENEES	43,574	25,670	49,577	45,616	38,758
NORD PAS-DE-CALAIS	41,142	30,603	43,235	44,470	42,035
PAYS DE LOIRE	35,520	32,635	33,429	40,007	38,527
PICARDIE	28,402	25,388	30,353	26,354	35,974
POITOU-CHARENTES	30,393	42,766	30,936	26,167	28,702
PROVENCE-COTE D'AZUR	82,148	57,204	74,526	91,203	102,658
RHONE-ALPES	61,252	23,978	60,634	68,470	64,230

For the period 01-10-2003 to 30-09-2004
Note: Data for Ile-de-France not included   **Source:** www.immoprix.com

Buying Property in France

example in the festival area would be approaching €24,000 after agents' fees,' Campbell says.

The value of property in Cannes has risen significantly, by 22 per cent in 2003, 12.1 per cent in 2002 and 14.2 per cent in 2001.

Conversely, if you want a property as your personal retreat, investment opportunities may be irrelevant. You can, for example, buy a small Normandy farmhouse to restore for as little as €11,000. It probably won't have much rental value and its value would be unlikely to soar, but it could be your perfect holiday home.

Unknown territory

If you are tempted to opt for an area you do not already know, exercise extreme caution. If property is very cheap, there may be an unpleasant reason for this. There may be problems, such as floods or social difficulties, in the area which may not be apparent on one visit. In any event, even if you think you know an area from visiting it on holiday, you should always do thorough research before committing yourself. Make yourself an expert on the area by studying as much literature as possible on it – books, magazines, local newspapers, internet sites. Get to know the differences between the country's 22 regions and 96 departments. Until you do, you will never be able to be sure that you have chosen the right area. Also, visit it as much as you can and at different times of year. A pretty river valley in the summer may be a raging torrent of floods in the winter.

The risks

As with any country, each area of France comes with its own risks and flooding is one of the most significant to watch out for. Even though floods have always dogged the country, over the last few years the situation has become worse. The south is one of the areas to be particularly cautious about, because the combination of the mountains together with the summer

How to find the right property

warmth and the moisture from the sea often creates dramatic storms. Winter in the area can be no less threatening. This does not mean you should not buy a property in the area, but when searching you should be especially vigilant. Look out for signs of previous floods, such as sandbags, ask the locals and check the local press (their websites may give you information from back issues relating to floods).

At the other end of the spectrum of weather risks is drought. Again, this does affect the whole country, but the area most affected is the north. Clay (*argile*) lies in the ground below many homes throughout the country and with a severe lack of water it shrinks and can cause structural damage. Forest fires are another hazard resulting from heat and drought, and these have occurred most dramatically recently in Le Var.

Other non-weather-related risks to look out for include the possibility of an earthquake in the Côte d'Azur and termites, which present a severe hazard to property in much of the country, but particularly in the south, south-west and west.

To find out about precisely how any of these issues might affect a property that interests you, you will need to get expert advice, but before you get to this stage – where you will be paying for someone to do your research – you should ask questions of as many people near to the property as possible. To do this, you will need to know something of the French language and, the more you know, the quicker you will be able to get to the truth. Locals will be far keener to chat to you in their own language than in broken English. It shows you have made some effort. Learn as much of the French language as you can. You might find it fun and it could save you a lot of time and money in the long run.

Ease of access

Ease of access will be another key ingredient in making your purchase a success. If you are buying for a holiday home, you will probably want to be within a certain travelling time from the UK. If this is the case, you will probably want to be near, but not too near, an airport or train station (probably the fast TGV). But do not rely on adverts claiming optimistic travel times. Just like British rail timetables, these can often turn out to be among the biggest works of fiction ever written. Try the route yourself as many times as possible before committing your money to the property. And ask other people in the area as well as the many estate and travel agents who will offer advice. Be careful of being too reliant on flights that are pioneering access to new areas. If only a handful of budget airlines fly to a destination, they may stop their services or hike their prices if the route proves uneconomic.

Of course, convenience comes at a price. 'The areas that are well connected, such as Nice, tend to be quite expensive,' says Patrick Dring, Knight Frank international residential division partner. 'This has advantages, though, such as great flights connections and being generally accessible with more ease, but the south-western areas, where there are not quite so many easy connections, tend to be cheaper. You may be able to get back some of your costs through letting your property, but don't be over-optimistic. People can generally expect a 20–25-weeks' letting season and, even though seasonal letting does not bring in a decent income, it can cover the costs of living, for example, and maybe leave a bit of pocket money to spend too,' Dring adds.

As well as considering general factors about regions and areas when you are on your search, when you find a property that interests you, consider everything carefully. Does it face the right direction? Is it near a current or planned busy road (which you should be able to check with the local *mairie*)? Will it get any sun? Will it be draughty? Will it be noisy (a nearby farm or church may be quaint, but a tractor revving or bells ringing at dawn every morning could quickly turn into a nuisance)? These are factors that are easily forgotten in the euphoria of finding a property you think is perfect.

There are numerous ways to find properties, from estate agents, agents who will, for a fee, look for a property for you, magazines and newspapers, but increasingly people are doing

How to find the right property

much of their preliminary work without even leaving their living rooms, on the internet. (See the Appendix for a list of sites.) One key website is the official site of the French government tourist office, Maison de la France (www.france guide.com). All these routes to finding your perfect home are useful, but beware of relying too much on any single source. Garner information from as many places as you can.

A case in point

One of the best ways to get information, of course, is to ask someone who has already done what you are hoping to do. Theatre manager Christopher Durham bought an old, large barn with attached house in rural Normandy in 2003. He intends to modernise it, because, at the moment, it has a living room, kitchen, two bedrooms and large attic, but no bathroom!

'We have lots of space (about 35 acres) of peace and calm, as well as a local community which readily accepted us, and a civilised way of life.' It cost €109,000 and would now sell for around €120,000. 'The only downside is the time spent travelling to and from the UK. The nearest airport (with limited flights) is an hour from the property and it is a six- to seven-hour drive from ports such as Caen, Le Havre and Dieppe.'

Durham found his property by touring two or three regions, viewing innumerable properties and, eventually, by having a chance conversation with a local farmer. The process was not that quick and it was rather 'frustrating', because he was buying an agricultural property, which can be more complicated, because of the stricter rules governing properties used for agricultural and or other business uses, Durham says. 'We viewed in August 2002 and October 2002, our offer was accepted in late 2002/early 2003 and we eventually signed in October 2003!' Durham explains.

But it has been worth it. 'The area is rural and quiet, the nearest small town (population 1,100) is about five miles

Buying Property in France

away and the area is mainly a French farming community with only a couple of British families owning property within a 15-mile radius. It provides the perfect antidote to high-pressure life in the UK and has absorbed all our available funds to date. It has given us the goal for early retirement. We have grown-up children, who, we hope, will enjoy visiting with grandchildren in the future.'

Durham says that if he were to go through the process again he would 'possibly drive a harder bargain'. To others about to take a similar step, he advises, 'Don't rush into a purchase any more than you would in the UK – remember that there are still more older properties available in France for 'restoration' than in the UK. From the outset be prepared: read as much as possible about France and the French, check all relevant information relating to the area you are considering, such as transport links, climate, access to facilities, research the various ways of financing a purchase and the different ownership options, consider taxation, inheritance, etc. Always remember that you are a visitor (short or long term) in the country.'

Top five things to remember:

1. Learn about French culture and the differences between the country's various areas.
2. Identify why you want the property – as a holiday home, investment, business?
3. Concentrate on a particular area that you can get to know well.
4. Find out about hidden risks, such as flooding, that there may be in the area.
5. Make sure that you will be able to get to your property easily. Check on flight/train/road connections.

CHAPTER 2
The letter of the law

Lawyers

You should get a lawyer in place and take his advice on what you intend to do before you start looking for your property. Once you find your ideal home, the seller may only allow you a limited time to proceed, or you could be racing with another buyer and if you have to spend an age arranging to see a lawyer you could lose your chance of clinching a deal.

'People buy different types of property in France, each implying slightly different legal issues,' explains Keith Baker, partner at Croft Baker & Co solicitors, who specialise in advice on buying in France. 'With skiing, the target property is usually an apartment, sometimes a chalet and the majority are off-plan. In this category what are known as sale-and-leaseback transactions have become very popular. For homes in the sunshine properties may be apartments or villas and there is an even balance between resale properties and off-plan. Rural properties usually have a large amount of land, need upgrading and sometimes have outbuildings with a view to providing B&B accommodation.'

Baker warns, 'What many people overlook are the inheritance implications of buying in France.'

Finding a lawyer is not a complicated process, but you will need to make sure that you have covered all the knock-on effects of your purchase. You will probably need a lawyer in your own country as well as in France, explains John Howell, senior partner at John Howell & Co solicitors, specialising in overseas property advice. 'Most UK buyers will need advice on issues such as who should own the property, how to minimise their French and UK tax liabilities, how to deal with the restrictive French inheritance system, whether a UK or a French mortgage is going to be best in their circumstances,' he says. 'The French lawyer will not be able to help with these issues, but whether you use an English lawyer or not you will also have to have the deed prepared and witnessed by the French notary.'

The best way to find your lawyer is through recommendation. If you have a trustworthy friend who has been through the process of buying in France, find out which lawyer he used and, of course, ask whether or not he was satisfied with the service.

If you find a lawyer through a recommendation, you should still check his expertise against recognised registers and make sure that he gives you a guide to his fees before you instruct him. The Law Society of England and Wales recommends certain registers, which will also give you details of lawyers if you can't get a recommendation from a friend. The Society itself has an online directory of solicitors listing qualified solicitors in the country on which you need advice. And it has listings of foreign lawyers practising in England and Wales. English and Welsh solicitors on the Law Society's Roll will have professional indemnity insurance and they will also be bound by a strict code of ethics. If you are employing a lawyer qualified in France, check that he has the necessary insurance to advise you and that he is suitably registered in France.

The French embassy will also have lists of lawyers who can help. Lawyers in France are known as *maîtres*.

The *notaire*

The *notaire* is a conveyancing lawyer who makes sure contracts involving real property are legal and he will

The letter of the law

authenticate agreements regarding the sale of land. He is governed by strict codes and liable to penalties if he makes mistakes. Like other lawyers in France, *notaires* are also known as *maîtres*.

Notaires are public officers and their charges are calculated on a scale fee (see page 24). They will also make sure that all the necessary searches and registrations are carried out and that any tax is paid. You can guarantee that you receive clear title (in other words, there will be nothing affecting the buyer's rights to the property) by paying for the property through their accounts. Even though you can check varioius matters, such as planning, yourself, it is advisable to ask the *notaire* to confirm these to minimise the risks of a misunderstanding.

In his role as a real property expert, the *notaire* will advise sellers and buyers on the process, including giving guidance on price. Buyer and seller can use the same *notaire* or they can each instruct their own, but the costs will be the same whichever route you choose. There may, however, be extra fees, beyond the fixed scale, if you require some specialist advice not generally associated with property transactions, such as guidance on setting up a business at the property.

For other, more detailed advice on businesses and other non-conveyancing issues you should speak to a specialist lawyer in the relevant subject.

The legal process

A *promesse* or a *compromis de vente* (the equivalent to the contract, which arrives some way down the line in the English system) begins the formal legal process of buying a property in France. But you need to be careful about what you sign, cautions John Howell. 'Generally, the process starts with either a formal offer to buy the property – in which case, if the seller agrees to sell, you will be committed to the purchase and will have to pay compensation if you do not proceed with

Buying Property in France

it,' he says. 'Or it begins by the signing of a contract to buy.' Either way, the buyer will be committed to buying the property, subject to a get-out clause and cooling-off period, as explained below.

The estate agent, not the *notaire*, may prepare the contract. Make sure your lawyer checks it thoroughly. Do not be lulled into a false sense of security because the contract comes at such an early stage. Remember, unlike in many other countries – where preliminary agreements with estate agents may not be binding – this early contract (*promesse* or a *compromis de vente*) in France is binding. Its terms may be negotiated at any stage prior to signature and there is not a legally-prescribed format that you can rely on as a guide, but it will need to identify the property clearly. It will contain the seller's warranties about his title, other terms of the sale, such as when it is to be completed, and, perhaps most importantly for the buyer, if you need to raise finance to buy the property you must make sure it contains some sort of get-out clause covering the possibility of you being unable to raise the money. Apart from in the circumstances defined in the get-out clause, the buyer will be bound to buy the property. A deposit, normally 10 per cent, is payable when the contract is agreed, the balance being payable at completion. The deposit should be paid to the *notaire*, whose responsibility it is to handle the formalities.

Before you sign the agreement, you must consider the ramifications of French inheritance laws (see below).

If you are not French, you will need to prove your identity by producing your passport, and married couples who want to own the property jointly may need to produce their marriage certificate.

Once you have signed the *compromis de vente* there is a seven-day cooling-off period, during which time the buyer, but not the seller, may cancel (rescind) the contract, but the buyer must use registered post (*lettre recommandée*). If the contract is rescinded, the deposit is returned to the buyer.

The letter of the law

After the signing of the contract, the *notaire* will carry out the necessary searches to make sure the property and the seller have all the rights as described by the seller.

To finalise the deal, the buyer will need to pay the *notaire* the remaining amount of the purchase price and any costs, charges and taxes. The usual methods for paying this would be by bank cheque or by bank transfer. Money to be paid from a bank or building society loan will be paid direct to the *notaire* by the lender. The parties must sign the deed of sale (*acte de vente*) in front of the *notaire*, who will then deal with registering the new ownership. After registration, the *notaire* will retain the deeds and an official copy (*expedition*) will be given to the buyer.

Buying off-plan

If you are buying a new property that has not yet been built, this is called buying 'off-plan' (*vente à l'état futur d'achèvement*) and different, stricter procedures apply to guard against the possibility of, for example, the financial failure of the seller before completion of the build.

The first stage in the procedure will be the option contract (*contrat de réservation*). For a deposit (usually non-refundable) not exceeding five per cent of the purchase price paid into a bank account closed to each party until after completion, the buyer purchases an option to buy a defined property (not just a non-specific unit on the building project). The option agreement will set out the details of the deal, including all the charges, the taxes (VAT (TVA) of 19.6 per cent, for example) and the price of the property.

The *notaire* will then ask the buyer if he wants to proceed with the option and send to the buyer copies of the necessary documents, such as the transfer and plans (*état descriptif de division* and *règlement de copropriété*). After the documents are received, one month is allowed for the buyer to decide whether to complete the deal or give up his deposit.

Buying Property in France

Certain key factors should be included in the documents, such as:

A 10-year warranty to cover structural faults, covered by insurance, and a warranty of two years covering non-structural faults.

There should be guarantees (*garantie d'achèvement*) confirming that the developer has the necessary finance to complete the build, provided either by a bank (*garantie extrinsèque*) or by the developer confirming the necessary financial requirements have been met (*garantie intrinsèque*).

When the transfer deed (*acte authentique de vente*) is signed the buyer owns the property and pays at least one third of the completion money. The developer will be able to take the five per cent deposit. After this, the buyer will pay for the property as the building work progresses, when the developer's architect issues a certificate confirming that enough work has been finished to warrant the payment.

After all the building work is completed, the buyer takes legal possession of the property (*remise des clefs*) when he pays the final instalment, which will usually be just a few per cent of the total price. Buyers should make sure to visit the building site throughout the construction process and then arrange insurance cover and inspect again before making the final payment.

Timeshares, common or part ownership

Timeshares in France, usually called *multipropriété*, are usually owned through an SCI (*société civile immobilière*, see below). In addition, in France a property may be part of a condominium agreement. This will divide up the property into different units (apartments and/or houses) and the document will describe how they are divided (*état descriptif de division*) and how the ownership works (*règlement de copropriété*). In a similar way to leases in the UK, but better defined, the agreement will allow the units each to be sold and owned by different people, there will be provisions to ensure that noise and other possible nuisances between units are controlled and duties regarding common areas, such as stairways and paths, will be clearly defined. There will also be a management company and details of the amount of management charges. If you are thinking of buying a property in such a scheme, ensure that your lawyer thoroughly checks all these documents and finds out about the service charges.

Leaseback schemes

These can cut the 19.6 per cent TVA tax on a purchase and there may be other savings, but the details of the scheme can be labyrinthine. Make sure you involve a lawyer from the start. The schemes generally work by a person buying a property and then immediately leasing it back to the developer, who will then usually allow the buyer to use the property for a certain amount of time each year. Properties bought in this way can often be difficult to sell.

Ownership decisions and inheritance law

Signing the *compromis de vente* will probably determine how you own the property, so great care needs to be taken at that early stage (see above).

French inheritance law is one of the main reasons for taking care. In France, a person's children have an automatic right to inherit a certain amount of property. In addition, ascendants – parents – also may be entitled to inherit. If you want to make sure that your wishes, rather than the will of the French law, prevail, you will need to address the type of property ownership you want to adopt. With careful planning problems can be avoided.

There are set legal rules for how much each person will inherit and in what circumstances. One child will get one half of the parent's estate; two children get two thirds shared equally between them and three or more are entitled to three quarters. If a person dies leaving no children, but one parent, that parent is entitled to one quarter of the estate. Two parents will be entitled to half the estate. Spouses are entitled to benefit from the estate only to the extent of what is left over.

Matrimonial property is dealt with in France in a different way from many other countries. It will be dealt with according to the parties' matrimonial agreement (in France, couples agree how they own their property on marriage) (which in the UK, for example, generally do not exist) or by the law (which stipulates that everything is owned communally – jointly between spouses). This can create problems, compounded by the inheritance rules related to children and parents. Clearly, the more times property passes from one person to another the more Inheritance Tax may be payable. To try to gain some control over what happens to their estate, many people use a number of devices, which may also save on Inheritance Tax. These include the *société civile immobilière* (SCI). This is an unlimited liability legal creation aimed solely at owning property. It is a type of company and will have a registered office, shares and most of the paraphernalia of a company.

If you use this scheme to buy your property, the company, not you, will own the property. Inheritance Tax can be minimised by giving shares to children during your lifetime. Because the human beings will own shares and not the actual property, the inheritance rules are different, covered by the law prevailing in the owner's country of domicile (which may well be the UK, for example) and so there is total flexibility in inheritance planning. There may also be advantages for tax, if you want to be governed by the tax system in your country of origin. You should, however, seek the advice of an accountant (*comptable*) to ensure that you do not have problems with a tax anomaly that treats people who own a second home through a company as receiving a taxable benefit in kind when they use the property.

The letter of the law

In addition, care must be taken, if you use this ownership method, to ensure that you do not become liable for Corporation Tax, which may kick in if, for example, you turn the property into a trade property by letting it furnished.

Christopher Durham, the case study referred to on page 9, bought his property through an SCI.

There are various other schemes for gaining control of inheritance, including *la clause tontine*. This states that the property is bought for the benefit of the surviving owner and the *notaire* will put this clause in the purchase document. When the first spouse dies, the child and ascendant inheritance rules will not apply, but Inheritance Tax may still be levied. If, for example, the owners are not related, the tax could be as high as 60 per cent. Married couples can also use the French marriage contract (*la communauté universelle*) to stipulate who inherits on the first death. It will apply to all property owned in France. By far the best way to deal with the inheritance issue is to own the property through an SCI, because it is the simplest.

It is probably a good idea to make a Will in France covering your French property, but you must take care that it does not conflict with any Will you may have in any other country. Take the advice of a lawyer who knows the laws of both countries.

Inheritance Tax

In the UK, the deceased's estate pays the Inheritance Tax based on the estate's value and then the assets are distributed. In France, each beneficiary pays the tax and the relationship between the beneficiary and the deceased, as well as value received, determines the rate paid. Widows, widowers and children pay a rate rising to 20 per cent on benefits up to a current figure of €520,000. There is then a sliding rate, rising from 30 to 40 per cent for higher amounts. There are various ways to minimise tax, including lifetime gifts, and to find out about these and tax applying to non-relatives you should take expert advice.

Buying Property in France

Top five things to remember:

1. Try to find a lawyer who has been recommended by someone you trust.
2. Take legal advice on your position before starting to search.
3. The *notaire* deals with the transaction for buyer and seller and you should take advice of a lawyer in your country of origin as well.
4. Do not sign anything without legal advice.
5. Consider inheritance and tax issues.

CHAPTER 3
Finance facts

Even though France is in many ways very different from the UK, in one respect, at least, it is the same. You will need money before you can do anything and to know what you will be able to do, you will need to know how much money you have to spend.

There are several different ways to raise the money you will need to buy your home from:

1. spare cash made available from your bank account or from the sale or mortgage of some other asset, such as shares;
2. a personal loan;
3. a mortgage on your current home to release equity from it for your French purchase; or
4. a mortgage on your French property.

Whatever you are thinking of doing, you should ask your bank manager, accountant and/or your financial adviser to help you. The first option is the easiest and probably the cheapest, but most people will have to look at one of the other possibilities.

'Purchasers need to know a good deal about the local conditions and legal restrictions in France before moving forward with their mortgage,' warns Conti Financial Services, which specialises in overseas finance advice. 'Lending criteria can often be quite different to what you might expect and there can be all sorts of knock-on effects on Wills and taxes, including Inheritance Tax.'

Buying Property in France

Personal loans, whether they are from a French lender or a lender in another country, will generally be at an interest rate that is not competitive with a mortgage. Unless you have no choice or you are particularly averse to putting a property at risk by securing a debt on it, the personal loan route is best avoided.

Generally, anyone buying a home in France will need to choose between borrowing by way of a French property mortgage (*hypothèque*) or a mortgage secured on a property elsewhere. You could also ask any lender on your current property to extend his loan, which would save legal and other fees.

Beware, though. If you buy a property in France and borrow the money for it in a currency from another country, this can present a risk if the currencies' relative values change significantly. If, for example, the currency of the lending country rises in value against the property's country, you could find that you owe far more than the property is worth. This can, of course, work the other way round, but you will, in effect, be playing a gambling game with currency markets.

Currency questions

It is also important to take into consideration the currency of your main income. For the same currency-fluctuation reasons, your income could end up being worth a lot less than your loan and your repayments relatively if your borrowing is in a different currency. The most risky option is to borrow in a currency different from both the currency of your income and the French property. A safe option is to borrow in the currency of your income, so that the relative values of your income and repayments will remain constant. Or, if you borrow in euros, and the foreign currency drops in value, at least the relative value of your French property in the foreign currency will simultaneously increase.

Remember, France's currency is now the euro, the value of which varies when compared with other currencies. At the time of going to press, one euro is equal to £0.685, but this

Finance facts

changes all the time and, if you have a loan of hundreds of thousands of pounds, fluctuations of £0.05 of a pound could cost you a lot of money.

When looking for the right lender, follow the same sort of criteria you would apply to any other mortgage: go for reputable, well-known names. Not all banks will offer mortgages for foreign property, but Abbey National, Barclays and the Woolwich do and Banque Transatlantique and Crédit Agricole are two French institutions used to dealing with overseas borrowers. Most lenders will need to check your financial worth and your employment position, as well as other details. Most institutions will give you an offer in principle, outlining how much they would be prepared to lend, before you find your property. This is worth obtaining, so that you know how much money you will have at your disposal before you fall in love with a property.

Apart from deciding on the institution you want to approach to lend you the money, you will need to bear in mind French law. A French bank is not legally allowed to offer a loan (by way of a mortgage or personal loan) if more than 30 per cent of your income will be consumed by the repayments. All of your financial commitments, such as other loans and rental payments, will be taken into account, but so will any joint income (money earned by one of your co-purchasers), up to a usual maximum of three borrowers.

With a loan from a French bank, there is an 11-day 'cooling-off' period after you receive the mortgage conditions document (*offre préalable*) to allow you to change your mind. The passport of anyone who will be a party to the mortgage must be shown to the bank. There are both fixed and variable-rate loans, but repayment mortgages only are available. You will need to repay capital and interest. In addition, you will usually only be able to borrow around 70 per cent, or perhaps a lesser percentage, of the value of the property on a French mortgage.

Buying Property in France

Mortgage offers

Mortgage offers have to be in writing, they must be accepted within 30 days and, within four months of the acceptance, the purchase must be completed. You need to keep your wits about you just as you would buying a property in your home country. If you commit yourself to a loan you cannot afford, you may end up losing your home.

The property purchase contract will set out if it is being bought with a mortgage and, under a procedure known as *la loi scrivener*, if the loan does not proceed, the purchaser should be able to avoid the contract and get back the deposit.

The costs

Remember, not only will you have to pay for the property, but you will also need to pay for the costs of buying it. You must take life insurance and when your loan is finalised, French banks make an administration charge (*frais de dossier*). As a rough guide, there will also be other costs, such as the following:

1. Transfer taxes and stamp duty. 7.2 per cent of the purchase price.

2. Land transfer fee. One per cent of the purchase price.

3. The *notaire*'s fees. These are charged on a sliding scale. For the first €3,000, the fees will be five per cent of the purchase price and this gradually reduces until there is a charge of 0.825 per cent for figures above €16,750. There are additional fees of 2.5 per cent of the amount borrowed for registering a mortgage on a French property at the *bureau des hypothèques* (register of mortgages). For selling a property, the *notaire*'s fees will be about one per cent of the sale price, depending on how much it is.

4. An English/Welsh lawyer's fees. To advise on how to tie your French purchase in with your UK affairs. The

Finance facts

charges will vary depending on exactly what advice you want. Obtain an estimate before instructing the lawyer.

The blow of some of these costs can be softened if your adviser helps you take advantage of one or more of the French tax breaks and grants. L'Agence Nationale pour l'Amélioration de l'Habitat, for example, may offer grants towards the costs of improvement of a building more than 15 years old, if it remains your principal residence for nine years after the work is completed. Other similar grants are available from the Direction Départementale de l'Equipement. You may also be able to claim tax relief on interest payments and on the costs of repair and renovation. There are also tax breaks for the costs of works related to renewable energy and insulation.

If you are resident in France, you may be entitled to help with buying your home. There is a scheme called '*Le prêt à taux 0%*', which may offer an interest-free loan up to €27,000 if a single person's net income is below €23,000 per annum or a family's net income is below €38,000. For some company employees, a scheme called '*Le prêt à 1%*' offers one per cent interest on loans of up to approximately €18,000. Other schemes are also available, including for retirement properties, and your adviser should be able to ensure that you take full advantage of them.

Do not forget that, just like in any other country, your spending on the property will not end when you take ownership. There are, for example, French property taxes.

The public revenue office (*trésor public*) in the local area will collect:

1. the *taxe d'habitation*. This is a tax paid by the occupier of the property, which will be usually be you. One of the few exceptions to you having to pay it would be if the property is on a long-term let from you. In any event, the tax is usually no more than about €100 per year.

2. *taxe foncière*. The owner of a house must pay this, which depends on the rentable value of the property. It will usually be about four times the amount of the *taxe d'habitation*.

There is also a wealth tax (*impôt sur la fortune*) of about one per cent, which you will need to pay if the value of your home is worth more than €720,000, including its contents. And if the value of your home rises, you may need to pay Capital Gains Tax (*impôt sur les plus values*) of 33 per cent on the amount of the increase, after allowing for renovation and rebuilding costs.

In addition, there will be the usual utility costs that you would have for a house anywhere, and buildings and contents insurance.

Top five things to remember:

1. Take advice from your bank manager, financial adviser or accountant to find out the best method of financing your purchase.
2. Consider the currency fluctuations before borrowing in one currency and buying in another.
3. Stick to mainstream, known, lenders if you can.
4. Don't forget the legal costs taxes related to your purchase when calculating how much money you will need.
5. Consider trying to obtain a grant if you are thinking of renovating.

CHAPTER 4
Checking your bricks and mortar

Once you have found a property that you could consider calling your home, the nitty-gritty work will begin. You would not buy a property in your home country without checking that it was not about to fall down and that what the sellers say is theirs does, in fact, belong to them, and you should certainly not fail to check these things in France. Different customs do, however, apply to inspecting and surveying a property in France compared with many other countries.

While in the UK, for example, it is usual to arrange for a surveyor to check a property before you buy it, a friendly builder will often give an estimate for necessary works to a property for many French people. Bear in mind, though, that these French buyers will often know the area intimately and may well have known the specific property for a long time. As a foreign buyer, you will not be in the same position and simply employing the services of a friendly builder is likely to be too risky. Whereas in, for example, the UK surveyors hold a virtual monopoly on surveying properties, this is not the case in France, where there are different professionals offering varying types of surveying services. These are described below.

You can, of course, use a surveyor from your own country. The advantage of doing this is that he will speak English, but the downside is that whoever you employ will be unlikely to have the same depth of knowledge of the French property

Buying Property in France

market and specific difficulties related to various areas of France as a French professional. If, however, you do choose to instruct a non-French surveyor, at least make sure that he is insured for the advice he gives related to France. If he is not and he makes an error, you could be left paying the cost.

Different survey options

At the most basic level, an estate agent (*agent immobilier*) will, for about €250, inspect the property. If you go down this route, use an agent independent of the selling agent and do not expect anything much more than a valuation. You will be unlikely to find out about any defects that are not already pretty obvious.

A step up from the *agent immobilier* is the *expert immobilier*. He works under a stricter professional code and will have professional indemnity insurance, which will cover you if he makes a negligent mistake. For about the same price as the *agent immobilier* charges, the *expert immobilier* will provide you with a report outlining the key factors relevant to the property. This is called *une expertise amiable et privée* and it will also venture a view on the price. For an extra €300, the *expert immobilier* will offer a much fuller report covering more detail on defects in the property in *un bilan de santé immobilier*. This is the more advisable route, especially where the property requires renovation.

A *notaire* may also offer a valuation, but this is likely to be very limited and mainly concerned with ensuring that everything is legally correct rather than structurally sound. In addition, master builders (*maître d'oeuvres*) will check properties that are more than about 60 years old, maybe for free, if they are going to do any necessary work, and an architect (*architecte*) will check more up-to-date properties.

As well as the structural issues, you must also make sure that the seller does, in fact, own all the property he is proposing to sell. This is particularly important in rural areas, where fences could have been moved easily, but it is also advisable even for

Checking your bricks and mortar

apartments in cities, to ensure they are, for example, as big as the agent's details suggest. For a fee, which will vary depending on the sort of work you require him to do, a *géomètre-expert* (a specialist in checking boundaries) will check all this for you.

New-home guarantees

Many of the worries of buying a property can be alleviated if you buy a new home. These will come with a 10-year guarantee (*garantie décennale*), so you needn't worry too much about making sure the building is sound, and, generally, it will not require any work for a long time. The guarantees are similar to the UK's NHBC scheme (which offers a 10-year guarantee, based on minimum construction standards). There are other attractive advantages as well, such as lower property taxes and better insulation, all of which will save you money. And, when you come to sell, you may find it easier than selling an older property. Unlike the UK property market, French buyers are less obsessed with period properties and modern homes are often easier to sell. The limited number of disadvantages include a VAT of nearly 20 per cent that is paid on the first sale of all homes of less than five years old.

You can also buy a property that has not yet been built – buying off-plan. This is not unique to France and there are some disadvantages, such as a nearly 20 per cent VAT on building costs and a different purchase procedure from already-built homes (detailed in chapter 2). Apart from this, there are many of the same advantages as buying other new homes.

If the property you are buying is old and previously renovated, find out whether it was a DIY job by the seller (in which case you should exercise extreme caution and insist on a thorough expert inspection) or if builders carried out the work (in which case ask to see their bills and check how long there is to run on the guarantees and warranties).

Buying Property in France

Co-ownership care

Many properties in France are co-owned by people living near each other. So, for example, in a block of apartments where the hallways are shared by the owners of all the apartments, the whole property may be co-owned. The same might be true of houses on an estate, whether they are detached or terraced. This system is called *copropriété*. If you are thinking of buying one of these properties, be careful to check the contribution you will need to make towards the upkeep of the common parts, find out about what the rules and regulations (*règlement de copropriété*) are and make sure it is run well. Service charges can be high in some developments, so it is important to find out exactly what they have been over the past few years and to check the controls residents have over how they are set. You can always speak to the other owners to find out how effectively the property has been looked after, but your lawyer should check all the details of the service charges.

From damp to termites

Other factors to bear in mind at this early stage for all properties include termites, asbestos, radon (a radioactive gas present in Brittany, the Massif Central and some other places), lead and damp inspections (mostly carried out by an *expert en techniques du bâtiment*, who specialises in checking many of the health aspects of a property). And, if the property has a swimming pool or septic tank (*fosse septique*), get it checked to ensure it comes up to legally-required standards and make sure there will be no obligation to connect the property to a sewer. New laws require some properties to be connected and if you end up having to do this, it could cost you a lot of money, perhaps many thousands of pounds (or, rather, euros). Also be sure that you will be able to do what you want with the property. Is it a listed building (*monument historique*), for example, or in a conservation area (*zone de protection du patrimoine*

Checking your bricks and mortar

architectural urbain et paysage)? In either case, the potential for changing the property will be severely limited. This information may be available at the local *mairie*, but you should ask the *notaire* to check it.

There are a number of checks you can do yourself about planning requirements and other matters, before you start to pay for professionals. At the most simple level, you can ask the seller to show you the deeds, to prove he owns all the property you want to buy and also to show what restrictions there may be on it. At the town hall check that the property is not in a flood zone (*zones inondables*) and that the local development plan (*plan local d'urbanisme*), which will show planned buildings, roads and the intended shape of the area, is to your liking. Anyone thinking of renovating, changing the use of a property or going into business in a property needs to take extra care.

If you are very brave, you may be considering buying a plot of land and building your own property. Needless to say, if you do this, be sure to find out the costs of the build and whether or not local planning laws will allow what you want before committing yourself to the purchase.

When you have finished dealing with all the major, legally-related issues, do not forget to check the everyday basics. Is the property connected to the water mains and if it isn't, where does the water come from, how good and old is the electric system, is there gas and where does it come from, is there a phone, does the line need updating and will you be wanting a fast internet connection if you will be working from home? Are structures, such as walls, sheds and barns, on the land sound? Being surprised by having to deal with any of these issues out of the blue could be very costly and aggravating.

At the same time as ensuring that all the buildings and structural matters are sound, you will need to get your lawyer to check that all the legal issues connected with the property are acceptable.

Buying Property in France

Top five things to remember:

1. Surveyors come in various shapes and sizes in France, but buyers should exercise caution and get the most thorough inspection.
2. Make sure any building work has proper receipts and guarantees.
3. Consider new-home guarantees.
4. Do not forget to check safety, boundaries and outbuildings, as well as the main building structure.
5. Make sure to check the basics, such as whether property is connected to the sewer.

CHAPTER 5
The renovation and build-your-own game

Many people buy to renovate or they may even buy their own plot of land to build their own home, but you must not forget that, just like anywhere else, France has planning laws and building controls governing extensions, demolitions and changes of use. In addition, if you will not be there during the work you will need to consider how you will manage builders from afar. Or, you may be brave enough to take on much or all of the work yourself, but you need to be sure exactly what you are capable of and how big the job is going to be. The precise requirements of planning law vary a huge amount, depending on the project, and it is essential to take the advice of a *notaire* or *géomètre* (surveyor).

The first thing to bear in mind, perhaps, is that whatever you plan to do, try to keep it sympathetic to the local style. Whatever you do to your house, you will need and want to get on with the locals. Do not start off by poking them in the eye with a building they hate. Ask them their views and let them hear yours.

When choosing builders, try to use people who are recommended by people you trust, perhaps your *notaire*, or friends who have renovated their own French properties. You should also try to use local tradespeople who are properly registered in France. They should have what is known as a Siret number (confirming TVA registration, issued by the Chamber of Commerce); *responsabilité civile*, covering the builder with insurance for damage to the house; and *décennale* insurance, covering a guarantee of workmanship for up to 10 years.

If you have plans for a property you are interested in buying, make sure you will be able to do what you want before you commit yourself to it legally. If necessary, ask the seller to get the necessary permissions before you proceed. If you must make any sort of contract before knowing whether planning and building will be allowed, make sure a clause is included in the preliminary contract confirming that the sale is conditional on the buyer getting the necessary permission (*clause suspensive*).

The process

It is always a good idea to speak with officials at the *mairie* to find out the sorts of schemes they will generally allow. This may avoid you going to all the expense and trouble of applying for planning permission, and having the related plans drawn up for something that would never be acceptable to the officials.

Some smaller works and particular projects, such as swimming pools, may require no permission. Before going ahead with anything, however, it is important to get your *notaire* or *géomètre* and/or the officials at the departmental planning office (*Direction Départmentale de l'Equipement*) to confirm that your plans do not need permission. Get this confirmation in writing, so that there can be no argument about it in the future.

Outline planning permission or an indication of whether building is allowed at the property (*certificat d'urbanisme positif*) will be needed if you want to change the outer appearance of your property significantly. You can either apply for a detailed permission (*certificat détaillé*), covering, for example, the style of the property or just apply for a simple certificate (*certificat simple*). Either the *notaire* or the *géomètre* can make the application at the town hall (*mairie*).

The renovation and build-your-own game

Officials at the departmental planning office will consider the application and, if they agree to it, the *mairie* will issue the necessary certificate. You must also find out the proportion of the land you will be able to use for building (*coefficient d'occupation des sol*).

Before starting the building work, ensure you have full insurance to cover it or any of the workers having an accident on your property (*dommage et ouvrage assurance*).

After a process that normally takes two months, you will receive the necessary certificate, which is valid for 12 months only. You must apply for planning permission (*permis de construire*) as soon as possible after receiving this initial certificate to ensure you do not run out of time.

The application for the *permis de construire* is sent to the town hall as well, but it will need detailed plans of what you intend to build. The town hall will write to you telling you when you should receive a decision and the officials will display your application. After you receive the permission, you have 24 months to start the work. You must get the go-ahead (*déclaration d'ouverture de chantier*) for actually starting the construction from the *mairie*. After you get permission and you want to start your build, you must put a sign outside the property giving details of what you intend to do and stating that you have permission. When the works are finished, you must apply to *mairie* for a confirmation that the building work conforms to the requirements of the permission (*certificat de comformité*).

If the size of the proposed building is 170m^2 or bigger, then an architect will have to apply for the planning permission. Different regulations cover agricultural property, such as farms and farm buildings. The regulations cover factors such as the types of crop that can be grown and whether or not farm buildings can be used for non-agricultural purposes. If a listed historical monument is near the property, you may also need to find out from the relevant officer for the locality at *l'Architecte de Bâtiments de France* (historic building specialist office) exactly what you can do at the property. You can also

Buying Property in France

check with the local officer of the *Conseil d'Architecture, d'Urbanisme et de l'Environnement* (architectural aesthetics specialist) about what might be allowed. Contact details of the officer relevant to the local area can be found in the Yellow Pages (*Pages Jaunes*).

Planning refusals

If a planning application is refused or you have been given permission, but subject to unreasonable conditions, it is possible to make revised application for planning permission to attempt to get what you want. Much like in many other countries, you have two months from the planning decision to take your application to a tribunal, which may decide that the original decision of the *mairie* was wrong. However, if you do win before a tribunal this is not the end of the matter. You must make another application for planning permission, although any new refusal or conditions cannot be the same as stated in the original decision.

Budgets and bills

Before even planning your build or, in fact, buying the property you must decide on your budget. Discussing any potential project with builders and other experts, such as *géomètres*, will help you determine what needs doing and how much it will cost.

Do not commit yourself to anything until you have quotes from builders and the other professionals giving you as close to a fixed price as you can get.

Unlike in the UK and many other countries, builders in France work to contracts, which should cover certain minimum factors, such as payment stages; penalty clauses for delays in the work by the builder and in payments for you (these would, for example, provide for reduced payments in the event of late completion); and full details of the building, including a construction schedule.

The renovation and build-your-own game

A payment schedule would, for example, state that you pay perhaps 10 per cent of the price for the job when you sign the contract and then the rest split up according to the completion of various other sections.

Throughout the build, as you pay, make sure to get a receipt each time and retain these for future reference. This may prevent any disputes with builders and receipts may be useful for future owners. When you are assessed for any Capital Gains Tax in either England or France, these receipts will also show your total expenditure on the property, to reduce any tax liability you may have.

Other factors

When you buy, check the basics, including the position for obtaining a supply of electricity, a septic tank (*fosse septique*) and water supply. Ask the locals for advice about what is and isn't possible and then double-check what they say with an official at the local *mairie*.

Land and building costs vary across France, as with any other country, but generally, essential tradespeople, such as plumbers and builders, will be more expensive in more upmarket areas, such as Paris, than cheaper rural areas, such as the countryside of Gascogne.

Of course, some are looking for even more adventure than renovating or building their own property in a foreign country. They may also want to set up business there. We deal with this in the next chapter.

Buying Property in France

Top five things to remember:

1. Try to find out as much as possible about local architecture and local feelings about building. This could save time and money in the long run.
2. Do not commit yourself legally before you know you can do what you want with the property.
3. Allow plenty of time to get planning permission.
4. Make sure you have insurance to cover accidents during the building work.
5. Discuss the potential costs of your plans with builders and other tradespeople before committing yourself to a project.

CHAPTER 6
Business property and letting

Many people buy properties in France with a view to setting up or buying an existing business (perhaps a hotel or bed and breakfast or a working farm or shop). Another popular money-making route for foreign buyers of properties in France is to buy a property as an investment, as perhaps a buy to let. Needless to say, there are laws and procedures governing planning and changes of use (converting from domestic to business use or vice versa), etc. for each option.

If your business idea will require any skills from you, are you sure you have them or can get them? Once you have committed yourself legally, it may be too late to do anything about it.

Before you get to the property-buying stage, however, there are other factors you will need to consider. 'The most important advice is to make a business plan (in English) and then to get detailed advice about your business idea and whether it will work in France as soon as possible,' explains solicitor John Howell, senior partner, John Howell & Co. 'Many ideas that might work in the UK will never work in France.'

There are many sorts of businesses that may appeal to people buying property in France, but one of the most common is buying as an investment. John Howell explains: 'As in any country, this is buying as a business.' If this is your plan, then, 'decide at the outset whether you want to have any personal use of the property or whether it is purely an investment, and you should get clear advice about the best type of property in the area where you are thinking of moving and get detailed advice as to the best ownership structure and tax control structure.'

Letting

Whether the property is partly your home or solely an investment, it is critical to be realistic about the sort of rental income you can expect. If you will be relying on the income, check with local letting agents and in local papers first before committing yourself to buying the property (see Appendix).

Some people buy a property and let it out fully or partly, all or some of the time as an investment or to pay for its upkeep. This can be achieved by buying the property outright and then doing as you wish, or through a leaseback scheme as mentioned in chapter 2.

French authorities will not usually regard letting your property (either wholly or partly, as, for example, a bed and breakfast) to earn extra money for the mortgage as a commercial enterprise, so there will be fewer rules and regulations. But if your property has six or more bedrooms, this will be treated as a business.

All let property must be registered with the local town hall. You must also register with the *préfecture* (Interior Ministry body at departmental level) if you are running a B&B or there are eight or more bedrooms. Even though small-scale rentals are not usually subject to an inordinate amount of regulation, you should seek the advice of your lawyer before embarking on the project.

For letting out your home in France (as a *gîte*, for example), you will need to be careful about any restrictions there may be in the ownership documents. Communal ownership schemes may, for example, have restrictions on letting out the property. You must always inform your insurance company that you are letting out the property, so that you can be sure that the policy will still be valid.

Business property and letting

There are certain minimum legal requirements for non-holiday letting property. Your agreement must, for example, be written and state whether it is a furnished property contract (*contrat de location de locaux meublés*). It is always advisable to check this document with your legal representative. Most letting agents, if you use one, will have their own standard form of agreement, but make sure it fits with what you want to do. All contracts must be read and signed by all parties to it, who must then state on the contract in French that they have read and understood it (*lu et approuvé*). If you are letting to non-French speakers, bear in mind that you may need the agreement to be in more than one language. Holiday lets do not give the tenant as much legal protection so the agreements need not be too elaborate (they are often not in writing), but whatever sort of arrangement you are anticipating, make sure to have any documents checked by a lawyer before using them.

As another precaution, make sure you make an inventory of what is in the property and take photographs of its condition, before letting it out. This ensures that if there is any loss or damage during a period when the property is let you will be able to hold the tenant to account. And, to this end, it is preferable to take some sort of deposit if you are agreeing to a long-term let. You must also make sure that there is someone available to cover possible emergencies, such as a burst pipe or malfunctioning machine. If your tenant has to do without essential equipment, you may end up losing rent or encountering more serious legal action.

You should also check into the tax ramifications (income earned in France may be liable to tax levies there). There are a number of different letting regimes on offer and the one you choose may affect the tax you pay on the income. The various schemes are split into furnished and unfurnished lettings:

Unfurnished lettings schemes are:

LMNP: if your annual income from rent is less than a certain amount, which you need to check at the time, you are not registered as a landlord and certain other conditions are met, you may be allowed to make a certain amount of income tax-free. Check this with your lawyer or accountant. The initials stand for *location meublée non-professionelle*.

LMP: this is similar to the LMNP, but covers registered landlords and includes potential exemptions from Capital Gains Tax. The initials stand for *location meublée professionelle*.

BIC and Micro-BIC: these are two separate schemes, both allowing for a percentage of tax allowance.

Furnished letting schemes include:

The Listed Building Scheme: enables you to set off loan or mortgage interest against tax, for example.

The Malraux Scheme: allows you to set renovation costs against all (not just rental) income, in certain circumstances.

Robien Scheme: similar to the Malraux Scheme, but it applies to new buildings as well as renovations.

Micro-Foncier Scheme: you may get an Income Tax allowance of 40 per cent for the expenses of letting if your annual rental income is less than a certain amount, which you should check at the time.

More details of these schemes can be obtained from the local Chambers of Commerce and/or your legal adviser.

Full businesses

If you will be operating a hotel or guest house from your property, this will probably be classed as a business. If you intend to do this or any other business at the property, it will be essential to find out if the local planning laws will allow it before committing yourself to buying. The procedures for this will be broadly in line with the planning process covered in chapter 5.

Business property and letting

You may, however, be considering buying an existing, operating business, which may have a home attached. If you are, you will usually find that there will be one price for the business value itself (*fonds de commerce*) and another price for the actual property (*murs*). You may even be buying a business without the property, if, for example, the business site is rented. In either case, make sure you take thorough legal advice. The business position may be critical for its success and a business rental property may not come with much security of tenure.

In addition to ensuring that the property site is adequately secure, you must ask an accountant to conduct a valuation of the business. Your legal representative/*notaire* (who will charge about 20 per cent of the purchase price) must also find out exactly what liabilities you will be taking on. Does the business have huge debts, for example? When buying a commercial premises and/or setting up a business, it is best to consult a specialist *conseil juridique* or *avocat*, even though the *notaire* will still be the person who must complete the *acte de vente*.

Lots of organisations will help you understand what is needed to establish a business in France, including the local Chamber of Commerce (*chambre de commerce et d'industrie*). French law requires every business to register (under threat of a fine or worse), no matter what it is. You will also need to ensure that you have insurance in place to cover yourself, your business and any staff.

To raise finance, if you need it, you will need to present a French bank with a business plan in French. You will need a similar plan if you want to get one of the many state loans or grants and a financial adviser specialising in French property should be able to point you in the right direction (see Appendix). Remember, you will need to make sure that your business has enough capital to operate, particularly if it is in a seasonally affected concern, such as tourism or farming.

Particular businesses attract special rules. Vineyards, for example, may be subject to planting restrictions relating to

Buying Property in France

certain varieties of grape. Farms may be subject to similar rules.

If you are setting up a business in France, you will, presumably, be moving there lock, stock and barrel, so you will also need to consider the migration issues, covered in the next chapter.

Top five things to remember:

1. Before you buy your property, check that legislation and planning controls will allow you to run your business from it.
2. Check that the business you want to run will pay for any finance you need to raise to pay for your property.
3. For letting property, ensure you use the correct documents and check the various ways to minimise tax.
4. For buying or setting up a business, you will need specialist legal advice from a business-law expert.
5. Do not forget the effect that running a business in France may have on your domicile status. You may need to ensure you comply with all immigration requirements.

CHAPTER 7

Emigrating to France

Some people may be considering plunging themselves into French culture more deeply than buying a holiday home. If you are considering emigrating to France, there is one central issue that will determine how your move progresses: are you a national of a European Union country? Apart from this, before committing yourself to buying a property, it is essential to check with the French authorities that you will be able to take up residence in and work or establish a business in the country. If you fail to do this, you may find yourself liable for a property without any means to pay for it. You may also consider renting before or while you settle the immigration issue and find a property to buy. In the short term this can be relatively simple and allow you to test the water for living in France before your decision is irrevocable.

French immigration rules

You must register with local authorities if you aim to stay in France for more than 90 days, and obtain a residence permit (*titre de séjour*). There are various permits, depending on exactly what you are doing in the country, including documents for members of your family (*membre de famille*). A permit for temporary residence (*carte de séjour*) is required for non-EU nationals and may even be needed for EU nationals. You can get a permit for permanent residence (*carte de résident*) after three continuous years of living in France, if you speak French. If you come from the European Union you simply need to apply for the necessary documents to ensure all the relevant authorities know where you are living. EU nationals have 90 days to find a job or get your business established.

For retiring to France, you will need to show the social security authorities that you have adequate funds to support yourself, whether or not you are from the EU. If, however, you are from the EU and you are a man retiring at 65 or woman retiring at 60, you are entitled to French social security benefits if you live in the country permanently.

Non-EU nationals will probably need both a visa and a residence permit. To ensure that you abide by time limits and that there can be no mistake with French customs officials, you should get an entry declaration (*déclaration d'entrée sur le territoire*) when you arrive in the country.

There may be harsh fines for not abiding by time limits and documentary requirements and, as with most countries, immigration and customs officials in France can be pretty tough. They may turn you away even if you look merely suspicious, without having to prove you have done anything wrong. Nicola Rogers, a barrister specialising in EU law, says: 'Police forces and government agencies increasingly share information from one country to another. People with no criminal convictions can often be stopped at borders or airports just because they are on a database for having been at, say, a peaceful protest. The current UK system for this sharing of information breaches EU law. It should only be used if there is a 'present and serious risk to one of the fundamental interests of society' (EU Directive 64/221).'

'UK nationals are at a disadvantage because the UK is not in the Schengen area of Europe (countries that have no border controls between them). This means they have to get into the Schengen area, unlike, say, a French national, who could get into Italy without a border control.'

Emigrating to France

Education and work

If you are considering working in France and perhaps educating your children there, John Howell, senior partner, John Howell & Co, has some good news. 'The jobs market is thriving for people with skills,' he says. 'The economy is booming, particularly in some areas. The cost of living is typically about 20 per cent lower than in Britain.'

If you do not already have a work or a business lined up, you should register with the employment office (*Agence Nationale Pour l'Emploi*) in your local area of France.

School admission criteria are relatively straightforward and largely depend simply on geography. If you are in the school's catchment area and it has a place available, you will be able to get your child in if you can prove your residence (with your official documents). You can enrol your child in the local school by visiting the head teacher or the *mairie*, depending on whether the school is independent or state run. The authorities will require your child to have received the necessary vaccinations and for this to be proved with his health card (*carnet de santé*).

Education facilities in France are generally good, ranging from means-tested crèches (available for children from two-months to three-years old) to a full system of schooling to take a child to his 18th birthday. Unlike some other countries, schooling in France is not compulsory for children under the age of six years old, although facilities are available before then if you need them.

Many French children go to assisted private schools, which are usually Catholic church institutions, where the teachers are paid for by the state. There are also state schools, where the standard of education is generally perceived to be better than, for example, their UK counterparts.

Often, non-French parents living in France choose to send their children to an international private school, although there are more of these available in and around city areas.

Buying Property in France

Fees can be high, many thousands of pounds per year. There are different nationalities of school available, including American and British, the latter more or less following the UK national curriculum. There are also international schools that are supported by the French state, so the fees are lower, but they may simply be an English-speaking part of a French mainstream school. This, of course, has its advantages, because the culturally-mixed environment might help your child ease into the French system. If you intend to stay in France long term, this might clearly be an advantage.

The French school year starts in September. There are several stages to the system: from six to 11 years old (*école primaire*); from 11 to 16 (*collège*), at the end of which there is an examination (*brevet*) and a report to decide on where your child will go next; 16 to 18, *lycée professionelle* or *lycée générale et technologique*, depending on your child's results at the end of *collège*. Children usually move up in the years throughout their schooling when they reach set standards of learning in their current year. This may mean they need to repeat a year. Afterwards there are universities or other educational establishments, depending on your child's career path, as with most other countries.

Other issues

There are other issues associated with emigrating, such as healthcare. These are dealt with in the next chapter.

Emigrating to France

Top five things to remember:

1. Before considering living France permanently, ensure that you will have enough money to support yourself.
2. Consider renting for a while before buying to test the water.
3. You may need to find a job or start setting up your business in France before you start living there, so that you do not face a period of unemployment.
4. Ensure you get the necessary permits, and visas, if relevant, or you could face a stiff fine.
5. If you have children, check that you get schools organised early, so that you maximise the chances of getting the school of your choice.

CHAPTER 8
What else should you consider?

Language and culture

To really get the full feel of the place, many people can't wait to turn Gallic. Christopher Durham, one of our case studies, has integrated into the French community. 'We have been thoroughly welcomed by one local French family and others probably find us curious,' he says. 'We have not experienced any antagonism or difficulties with any French we have encountered. We had a basic knowledge of French with a vocabulary which has grown over the years, particularly as I had previously purchased a property in Normandy. The principal cultural difference is that we are in a typical rural patriarchal society.'

When buying a property, you should be sensitive to the different local sensibilities. Rural areas may have a quite conservative outlook, so if you want wild parties, perhaps you should make sure your house is well away from everyone else or buy somewhere else. Some towns and cities, such as Marseille, may have religious or ethnic tensions.

Knowing the language is always a big help, even if you are buying only a holiday home. But you should be aware that the language varies depending on the region. People in Corsica will speak Corsican, in the Alsace people speak Alsatian and in the Basque country there is yet another variation. Many towns and cities will have language schools specialising in the variation appropriate to the particular region, so you can learn once you arrive. It would, however, be a big advantage if you learn it before you even start looking for a property. It will help you understand details better and it will also mean you can ask locals to tell you exactly what the truth is about their area and the property that interests you.

Health issues

If you were going to choose a country for its healthcare you could do a lot worse than France. The World Health Organization figures has judged the country's healthcare system to be the best on the planet. There is an emphasis on preventive medicine.

For ensuring you have healthcare cover for a visit to France, check with the post office for the relevant forms to complete. If you are working in France and living there on a permanent basis, you should register with the French state for its social security cover (check the Public Service website www.service-public.fr).

There are charges for medical appointments, but the fees are generally not much more than €20 to €30. Look out for the vast majority of *conventionné* doctors (like GPs). Their fees should not be too high. The state health system covers most charges and will refund the costs of hospital treatment. If you are included in the French healthcare scheme, you will receive a card (*carte vitale*) that enables any charges to be made and reimbursed, where relevant, by the state. There is virtually no such thing as a waiting list to see a consultant and you have the legal right to choose the doctors and consultants you want. Children receive a health card (*carnet de santé*), which will detail all their medical history.

Pets

A lot of us have a much-loved dog, cat, gerbil or other pet that

What else should you consider?

just couldn't be left out of a trip to France, but what are the rules for bringing animals into the country and looking after them when they are there? As with many things, the rules on this tend to be stricter in France than in the UK. While you are living in France you will need to make sure the pet has all its vaccinations and a pet passport, proving that the animal has had all necessary vaccinations, will be needed before you can take the animal into the country. For information on bringing pets and animals in and out of the country, contact the *Sous-Direction de la Santé et de la Protection Animales* at the Ministry of Agriculture www.agriculture.gouv.fr. Details of pet passports available from Britain can be found at www.defra.gov.uk.

You will need a licence to bring certain animals into the country, so check with the authorities first if you own something exotic. But for the usual family pets, such as cats and dogs, you should simply need to ensure they have their necessary health treatment and passport.

If you own a dog that was born after the start of 1999, you may need to ensure that it has some form of identification number in the form of a tattooing (*tatouage*) or a skin-implanted microchip (*puce*).

Working in France and the tax system

If you will be working in France, you should seek the advice of an accountant and/or a financial adviser who specialises in French finance.

If you are a European Union national, you have the right to work in France or anywhere else in the EU. Other nationals are likely to need permits. Jobs are advertised in many papers, but you will almost certainly need to speak French.

For employees, there is a minimum wage and you will be employed either on a fixed term (*contrats à durée déterminée*) of up to nine months or ongoing (*contrats à durée indéterminée*). Employment regulations in France tend to

Buying Property in France

give employees more security than in many other countries, such as the UK, but this does not mean you cannot be dismissed. Justifiable reasons for firing an employee would include behaviour that amounts to gross misconduct (theft, for example) and other factors that would be familiar to employees in many other countries. If you think you have been dismissed unfairly, you can take your case to a tribunal (*Conseil des Prud'hommes*). There may be strict time limits that govern your rights to make a claim. If you feel aggrieved, seek legal advice or the help of your trade or professional body as soon as possible.

You will be liable for Income Tax if you are living or working in France for 183 days or more. Everyone declares their own income (in a *déclaration de revenus*) and is responsible for settling their own tax. Each year, you must send details of your year's earnings to the public authority office (*hôtel des impôts*) dealing with tax for your local area. Spouses' incomes are dealt with together and charges to tax vary depending on the size of your family and your responsibility for dependants. After taking these factors into account, you are allowed to earn a few thousand euros per year without paying tax and after that there are rising bands with a top rate of tax of around 48 per cent.

If you run your own business and/or you employ anyone, be aware that you may have to abide by a whole array of employer regulations and rules far more extensive than in, for example, the UK. You should take legal advice to minimise the risk of making serious mistakes. Even if you do not employ people, you will have to observe minimum conditions related to insurance and other factors.

If you work for yourself, you will also need to pay tax (*taxe professionelle*) of up to about 20 per cent of an 8 per cent chunk of your VAT-inclusive (TVA-inclusive) income in respect of your business premises. This will still be payable even if you work from and pay the usual property taxes associated with your home. You are, however, entitled to reductions in this linked to the amount of business use of

What else should you consider?

your home. You should ask your accountant to check for other possible exemptions.

Selling your French property

The two main groups of professionals who can advise you on selling your French property will be estate agents and *notaires*. You should shop around to find an agent whose charges (usually anything up to a staggering 10 per cent of the sale price, plus TVA tax) you find reasonable. You can also negotiate when you find someone you think may be able to market your property successfully. Price should not be your only concern, though. If you feel one agent has a more professional approach or extensive marketing machine than another, this may mean that he will sell your property for a higher price or more quickly, although sales in France do not usually proceed particularly quickly.

Once you have settled on an agent, you will need to decide what sort of agreement you want to make with him. A simple agreement (*mandat simple*) would enable you to instruct more than one person to market your property or, indeed, usually to sell it yourself. An exclusive arrangement (*mandat exclusif*) ties you to one agent for as long as three months.

Before completion, make sure you write to all the utilities suppliers (gas, electricity, water, telephone) for final bills up to the date of completion. Other payments, such as property tax (*taxe foncière*), may be apportioned between you and the buyer, but you must inform the relevant authorities so that they can amend their records. Until the *acte de vente* (completion) you must carry on insuring the property. If you do not maintain the policy and the property is damaged, you will probably be responsible for paying for any repairs or you may have to reduce the sale price accordingly.

If your French property is a second home, you will be liable to pay Capital Gains Tax (*impôt sur les plus values*) on any increase in value since the date you bought it, with allowances made for building costs of renovating it and other similar expenditure. The usual rate is 26 per cent, but there may be reductions if you have owned the property for a lengthy period. The transaction will not attract the tax if you are selling your principal residence (a property you have occupied for five or more years), or you have owned the property being sold for at least five years and your principal residence is rented. Your *notaire* will collect the tax and detail this and all his other outlay in a financial statement before completion. You must tell the tax authorities in your country of origin about the sale. You may be liable for tax in your country of origin, but in some countries, such as the UK, there are double tax treaties which mean you may not have to pay two lots of Capital Gains Tax on the sale.

You should also be aware that if you are selling a property within five years of it being built, you will be liable to pay TVA at 19.6 per cent on the difference between the net sale and net purchase prices. After completion, make sure you get the sale funds from the *notaire* as soon as possible, because he is not liable to pay interest on any money held.

Top five things to remember:

1. Ensure you have adequate health cover.
2. If you have a pet, you must make sure its vaccinations are up to date and it may need a pet passport.
3. Take care when taking on any employment, so that you pay the necessary tax and get all your rights.
4. Watch out for estate agents' commission and Capital Gains Tax when selling your property. You may be entitled to relief against the tax.
5. Learn the language!

CHAPTER 9
Case studies

Professional advice is essential when buying any property, but sometimes the concern with legal red tape and bureaucracy can obscure the things that will matter more to most buyers, such as how long it took to find the right property, how long the process took, what life has been like with the locals. The best way to find out about these realities of buying a home in France is to ask people who have done it. Their stories may not tell you what always happens, but it is always heartening to know that other people have been through the process and survived.

Case study 1

Tom Sullivan and his business partner Guy Jeremiah bought two apartments in central Paris. They own one each. Both are part of apartment blocks and one of the buildings is about 100 years old, while the other is about 300 years old. 'We made sure there were no restaurants or retail spaces on the ground floor,' Sullivan says.

One apartment (measured in metres, as usual in France, is 36 sq metres) has one bedroom and the other is a studio apartment (24 sq metres). Both have one bathroom. One is in the Marais opposite the Picasso museum; the other is in Montorguiel, north of Les Halles.

'We bought both properties last year,' Sullivan says. 'We wanted to be able to use them ourselves and generate rental income. We wanted to create an alternative to central Paris hotels,

Buying Property in France

which are very expensive and very cramped.' His average let is for four or five days. The apartments are let about 60–70 per cent of the time so they can use them too.

'We bought the properties because we loved Paris and euro based mortgages were cheap,' Sullivan says. They reckon they can rent apartments 52 weeks a year in Paris whereas holiday homes elsewhere are only rentable 12 weeks a year.

It has changed Sullivan's life. 'I spent half of my life in Paris last year and really got to know the city,' he says. It is a far cry from his previous life as a Group Financial Controller. He is now self-employed, partly as a futures trader, partly with his wife's shop in Brighton and partly with a company called Europad running Paris apartment bookings.

He has a daughter, Alice (five months old). She has stayed in the Marais apartment. 'My wife has to do the trade shows in Paris every six months (prêt-à-porter, etc.) and it is now easier for us to go together. Having a base in Paris is really helpful.'

Even though Sullivan is more than pleased with his property, he does have some words of warning. 'Trying to manage the refurbishment remotely was taxing, especially as my French is not great. The building work took a lot longer than expected.'

Finding the right properties was quite hard work, but Sullivan was methodical. 'We picked certain areas and then went to every estate agent we could find. There was a lot of footwork, but *Le Figaro* online has a useful property search which covers all of France.'

'The process was very clear. Once an offer was put in and accepted we paid 10 per cent up front. Because one notary acts for both parties you know they are neutral. Also both parties meet each other on completion so questions can be raised direct with the owner. The process took about three months, which is the same as the UK. Fees (especially estate agents' fees) were high, though.' On the first apartment the basic price was €139,000, the estate agents' fees were €7,000 and *notaire* fees were €10,000 (including taxes, etc.).

Case studies

He has some advice for other buyers. 'Organise the mortgage at the same time as buying the flat. We bought in cash and then mortgaged afterwards, but it took a long time and we got hit by some fees. Spend more time than us looking at builders before starting any renovation work. The relationship with the builder is so crucial especially if you are in the UK for much of the time. Look at as many properties as you can. You start to get a feel for what is or isn't value for money. With apartments, watch out for annual service and maintenance charges – they can be high and you should know what they are.'

Both apartments cost in the region of €139,000 and about €22–30,000 was spent on refits. Property prices rose by an estimated 15–20 per cent in Paris in 2004, but Sullivan certainly does not intend to sell. 'We are more interested in the rental income. We see the value of the apartment itself as a long-term benefit (retirement!).'

Case study 2

Grant, 47, and Sandra Endersby, 43, bought an old manor house built in 1830 in need of a little love and attention and it is now their permanent home.

It has four bathrooms, four living rooms, seven bedrooms, three kitchens and a cellar. The Endersbys paid €185,000 for the manor with five acres of land and all the outbuildings in 2004. They spent €100,000 on renovations and one year later they reckon it would probably sell for around €350,000 to €400,000.

The manor (*manoir*) is in a pretty and small rural village, Maffrecourt, in the Champagne-Ardenne region, set in breathtaking countryside a few minutes from the edge of the Argonne forest. 'It is a charming, friendly farming community, who have been very welcoming and not a Brit or ex-pat within a 100 miles!' Grant says.

Buying Property in France

'We completed the purchase in April 2004,' explains Grant. 'We bought it for many reasons, but essentially we wanted to share the peace with guests in search of some tranquillity. We are developing a number of '*gîtes*'. The first is a self-contained two-bedroom apartment within the *manoir*, with private entrance; the second is in a building adjoining.'

Finding the property proved not to be too difficult. They prepared a wish list in French and emailed, posted and faxed it to a large number of agents in the towns that most interested them. Having already decided they wanted to live in the Champagne-Ardenne, it was just a case of finding the right property, in the right condition, with the scope, land and price they wanted! 'A relatively small number of agents replied and one of them was superb,' Grant explains. They visited three properties within a day, but knew the second one they saw was the one. 'You get a feeling, you just know. We were expecting to have to look at a large number of properties to find the one, but we were lucky.'

Having found the property in October 2003, they made a lot of visits and the previous owners are still good friends. The whole process took four months, but they were shrewd. 'We had good financial advisers and lawyers. When buying in France you'd usually be responsible for the agents' costs, but we negotiated with the vendor that he would pay these. Agents' fees in France are also considerably more than in the UK, sometimes more than 10 per cent of the property's value, so attention is needed in this regard.'

'The buying process is much better than in the UK, but we were terrified a piece of the puzzle might not fit. We did enjoy the meeting at the *notaire*'s office, though, when signing the final papers. Everyone concerned with the purchase was there and at the end we were given our keys. A great experience.'

Even though the area is very rural, the Endersbys made sure the property was easily accessible. It is within five minutes of the autoroute. 'We wanted to find a real French home, near enough to the UK to enable us to see our respective children (five between us: Sandra has Jessica, 17, Paul, 19 and I have

Case studies

Katie, eight, Victoria, seven and Thomas, three) on a regular basis, often three times a month.'

'The children have their own rooms and personal space to read and draw and the space in the garden to roam in a free open-country environment exploring the garden and the wildlife. We also liked the region for the warm summers and the rural village life in a French non-ex-pat community.'

'We are very happy and content with our new, more relaxed way of life with the tranquillity and peace. We now sleep better than ever before and I have lost over two stone by eating better French food, taking more exercise working in the grounds on tree maintenance and helping the artisans with the renovation work.'

Grant owns two small businesses in the UK, a web-design company and a specialist technical news agency. He runs them both from France with the help of colleagues in the UK and Finland. Sandra looks after the *gîte* business.

Having lived there for a year they still wake up each morning and look at the view and think how lucky and privileged they are. They got married there in 2005 this year in the local *mairie*, which is opposite their house. Their friend, the mayor, conducted the service and everyone in the village (Maffrecourt) came to the ceremony.

The only complaint they have is that builders were not that reliable and the renovation and *gîte* work was 12 weeks behind at one point. 'I know it's not unique to France, though,' Grant points out.

They are not holding back from getting involved in local life. 'We absorb ourselves in many of the local customs. Everyone stops for lunch from noon until 2pm and you'll see tractors discarded in fields mid-plough. When you go to a cafe or bar everyone says bonjour or bon appétit to those already enjoying their lunch and when we first visited the doctor's surgery everyone arriving also greeted all of those already in the waiting room. When joining a conversation or when meeting someone for the first time that day, everyone shakes hands or kisses with greetings of bonjour. It's very genuine and very civilised and we enjoy the politeness of everyone regardless of status. We have been learning French by throwing ourselves in at the deep end. If you make the effort, people will understand and one of our close friends and neighbours now feels comfortable correcting us when enjoying a glass of pastis in the evening.'

Grant's advice for others considering buying property in France is, 'Research the property and the area, use the right specialists for mortgage and legal advice, do a Will. Don't be afraid to make the move; it can be wonderful.'

Glossary

abonnement (m)	A subscription or regular charge for something
acompte (m)	A deposit
acquéreur (m)	A buyer
acquérir	To buy, acquire
acte authentique (m)	An official record in a document prepared by a *notaire*
acte de vente (m)	A conveyance in a document prepared by a *notaire*
agent immobilier (m)	An estate agent
agrandissement (m)	An extension
appartement (m)	A flat
arrhes (f)	A preliminary deposit paid by a purchaser
assurance multirisques habitation (f)	A home insurance policy covering all risks
attestation de comformité aux règles de sécurité (f)	A certificate of conformity to safety standards
avocat (m)	A lawyer
bail (m)	A lease
bailleur (m)	A leaseholder
bastide (m)	A country house

Buying Property in France

bâtiment (m)	A building
biens mobiliers (m)	A property that can be moved.
bilan (m)	A survey
bricolage (m)	Construction wares and do it yourself
bureau de vente (m)	A sales office
cadastre (m)	A registry
carnet de santé (m)	A book of medical records
carte de séjour (f)	A permit allowing residence
certificat d'urbanisme (m)	A permit for town planning
champ (m)	A field (piece of land)
chaudière (f)	A boiler
chauffage (m)	Heating
clause particulière (f)	A special condition
clause pénale (f)	A clause imposing penalty for non- or late performance of a contract term
clause suspensive (f)	A contractual condition upon which the agreement depends
commission comprise (f)	Includes commission
communauté (f)	A community or a husband and wife's joint property
commune (f)	A district
compromis de vente (m)	A land or property contract
comptable (m)	An accountant
conseil juridique (m)	A legal adviser
contrat (m)	A contract
copropriété (f)	Co-owned property
décennale (f)	A 10-year guarantee
demeure (f)	A home, usually a large abode

Glossary

département (m)	A geographical area of administration, similar to a county
dépôt de garantie (m)	A rental or purchase deposit paid
devis (m)	An estimate for property work
domaine (m)	An estate (land)
droit de passage (m)	A right of way
droits d'enregistrement (m)	Property purchase stamp duty
duplex (m)	A two-floor apartment
émolument (m)	Remuneration or fee
état hypothécaire (m)	A search at the land registry
expertiser	To value property
ferme (f)	A farm
fosse septique (f)	A septic tank
frais (m)	Fees
gardien (m)	A person who looks after the property
géomètre-expert	A surveyor of land
grange (f)	A barn
hôtel de ville (m)	A town hall in big town or city
hôtel des impôts (m)	A tax office
humidité	Damp
hypothèque (f)	A mortgage
immeuble (m)	A building
impôt sur les plus values (m)	Capital Gains Tax
inventaire (m)	An inventory
jardin (m)	A garden
jouissance libre (f)	Vacant possession
lotissement (m)	A housing estate

Buying Property in France

maçon (m)	A skilled builder
mairie (f)	A town hall in a small urban area, such as a village
maison (f)	A house
maison de campagne (f)	A house in the country
maison individuelle (f)	A detached house
maître (m)	An official title for a lawyer
mandat exclusif (m)	A sole estate agency agreement
mandat simple (m)	An aqreement with an agency allowing you to instruct other agents or sell the property yourself
médecin conventionné (m)	A health service doctor
menuisier (m)	A joiner or carpenter
mètre carré	A square metre
montant (m)	The total amount
monument historique (m)	A building listed as being of architectural interest. As in many other countries, strict planning rules apply to these buildings and properties near to them
notaire (m)	A conveyancing lawyer
permis de construire (m)	Planning permission
pigeonnier (m)	A pigeon house
prairie (f)	A meadow
préfecture (m)	The capital city of a department and also its Interior Ministry representative body, headed by a *préfet*
presbytère (m)	A vicarage

Glossary

promoteur (m)	A property developer
propriétaire (m)	A landowner/homeowner
quartier (m)	A distinct section of an urban area
règlements de copropriété (m)	Apartment or communal block rules
remise (f)	Storeroom, tool shed
remise des clefs (f)	When keys are handed over
terrain constructible (m)	Building land
testament (m)	A Will
SCI (Société civile immobilière) (f)	A company used for owning property
taxe d'habitation (f)	Occupancy tax
taxe foncière (f)	Property tax
tontine (f)	Ownership by more than one person where the survivor inherits the deceased's share on the co-owner's death
TVA (taxe à la valeur ajoutée) (f)	Value added tax – VAT
urbanisme (m)	Town planning

Appendix

Useful organisations and websites

This is not an exhaustive list. It covers some of the more helpful and significant organisations and businesses, but you should do your own research to find the people you find most helpful. In contacting many of the businesses and organisations in the list or buying any of the publications, you will find further links and resources.

Business/work

Fédération Nationale des Sociétés d'Aménagement Foncier et Etablissement Rural (SAFER)
Website: www.safer.fr

It has details of SAFERs around the country. It advises on setting up and buying farming businesses.

Franco-British Chamber of Commerce and Industry
31 rue Boissy d'Anglas
75008 Paris
Tel: 00 33 1 5330 8130
Fax: 00 33 1 5330 8135
Website: www.francobritishchambers.com

Lots of advice and contacts as well as advice and information on education and courses that might help your business.

French Chamber of Commerce
21 Dartmouth Street
Westminster

Buying Property in France

London SW1H 9BP
Tel: 020 7304 4040
Website: www.ccfgb.co.uk

Trade Partners
Website: www.uktradeinvest.gov.uk

There is lots of information on investing abroad on this site, sponsored by the UK government.

Diplomatic/public guides

British Consulate in Paris
Consulate-General in Paris
18 bis, rue d'Anjou
75008 Paris
Tel: 00 33 1 4451 3100
Fax: 00 33 1 4451 3127
Website: www.amb-grandebretagne.fr

British Embassy in France
333 rue du Faubourg
St Honoré 75383
Paris Cedex 08
Website: www.amb-grandebretagne.fr

French Embassy UK
58 Knightsbridge
London SW1X 7JT
Tel: 020 7073 1000
Website: www.ambafrance.org.uk

French Tourist Office
Website: www.franceguide.com

As much information about France, its culture and its various regions as you could want to get your search for a property started.

Appendix

Education/learning about French lifestyle and moving

Accueil des Ville Françaises
Head Office
62 rue Tiquetonne
75002 Paris
Tel: 00 33 1 4770 4585
Email: avf.paris@wanadoo.fr

Offers links to cultural and general organisations that can help you get to know your area of France and fit in with its lifestyle.

Alliance Française
1 Dorset Square
London NW1 6PU
Tel: 020 7723 6439
Website: www.alliancefrançaise.org.uk

Leading French language teaching.

Association France-Grande-Bretagne
Website: francegrandebretagne.free.fr

Anglo-French cultural organisation that aims to foster links between nationals of the two countries.

Francegate
Website: www.francegate.com

Useful information on French schools and cultural links.

Relocate France
17 Highlands Court
Highland Road
London SE19 1DR
Tel: 020 8761 9076
Website: www.relocate-france.co.uk

Runs seminars of expert and practical advice to help you plan for the French property-buying process and integrate into your local community.

Buying Property in France

Estate agents

Beaches International Property Ltd
3–4 Hagley Mews
Hagley Hall
Hagley, Stourbridge
West Midlands DY9 9LQ
Tel: 01562 885 181
Fax: 01562 886 724
Email: info@beachesint.com
Website: www.beachesint.co.uk

Currie French Properties Ltd
2 Fulbrooke Road
Cambridge CB3 9EE
Tel: 01223 576 084
Fax: 01223 570 332
Email: info@curriefrenchproperties.com
Website: www.french-property.com/currie

Destination France
Website: www.destination-france.co.uk

French Property Sales
Website: www.frenchpropertysales.co.uk

Apartments and villas in the South of France/Alps.

French Property Service
Tel: 01206 252 087
Website: www.frenchpropertyservice.com

FrenchProperty.com
Website: www.french-property.com

Knight Frank International Residential Department
20 Hanover Square
London W1S 1HZ
Tel: 020 7629 8171
Fax: 020 7629 1610
Website: www.knightfrank.com

Appendix

Laforêt Immobilier
Head Office
24 rue Jacques Ibert
92300 Levallois Perret
Tel: 00 33 1 475 9255
Website: www.laforet.com

One of France's biggest estate agencies.

Latitudes French Property Agents
Grosvenor House, 1 High Street
Edgware
Middlesex HA8 7TA
Tel: 020 8951 5155

Med & Mountain Properties
Website: www.medandmountain.com

Specialises in the Eastern Pyrenees.

Prestige Property
Website: www.prestigeproperty.co.uk/chateau

VEF
Website: www.vefuk.com

New-build specialists.

Exhibitions/fairs/shows

French Property News exhibitions/fairs
Tel: 020 8543 3113

Homes Overseas
Head Office
1st Floor, 1 East Poultry Avenue
London EC1A 9PT
Tel: 020 7002 8300
Email: jw@blendoncom.com
Website: www.blendoncommunications.co.uk

A major organiser of international property shows throughout the year.

Buying Property in France

The International Property Show
7 The Soke
Alresford
Hampshire SO24 9DB
Tel: 01962 736 712
Fax: 01962 736 596
Email: ian@internationalpropertyshow.com
Website: www.internationalpropertyshow.com

Shows are organised at different times of the year.

Finance/banking/insurance

Abbey National
Website: www.abbey-national.fr

Andrew Copeland International Ltd
230 Portland Road
London SE25 4SL
Tel: 020 8656 8435
Fax: 020 8655 1271
Email: roy@andrewcopeland.co.uk
Website: www.andrewcopeland.co.uk

Covers a host of insurance issues for anyone buying in France, as well as other countries.

Barclays
Website: www.barclays.fr

Call on freephone 0800 917 0157 from the UK, 0810 060 660 local call from France, or 00 33 1 5578 7030 from anywhere else in the world.

Conti Financial Services
204 Church Road
Hove
East Sussex BN3 2DJ
Tel: 01273 772 811
Fax: 01273 321 269
Email: enquiries@mortgagesoverseas.com
Website: www.mortgagesoverseas.com

Appendix

Specialists in financial advice for overseas.

Crédit Agricole Britline
Tel: 00 33 2 3155 6789
Website: www.britline.com

The banking branch of Crédit Agricole of Calvados, one of the regional banks of the Crédit Agricole group, which has 8,000 branches around France.

It is based on a telephone and internet banking service and dedicated to English-speaking customers.

French Mortgage Connection
20 Park Road
Fordingbridge
Hampshire SP6 1EQ
Tel: 01425 653 408
Fax: 01425 655 221
Email: info@french-mortgage-connection.com
Website: www.french-mortgage-connection.com

UK based mortgage brokers, who arrange mortgages with banks in France for buyers requiring one to buy in France.

International Buyers Department
70 rue Saint Sauveur
59046 – Lille Cedex
Tel: 00 33 3 2018 1817
Fax: 00 33 3 2018 1855
Email: ukbuyers@abbey-national.fr
Website: www.abbey-national.fr

Totalplanet
Website: www.totalplanet.co.uk

Advice on overseas investment.

Lawyers/surveyors

Chambre des Notaires
Tel: 00 33 1 4482 2400
Website: www.paris.notaires.fr

Buying Property in France

A *notaire* professional association. The website carries useful advice in French and English for buyers of properties in France.

Croft Baker & Co
Riverbank House
1 Putney Bridge Approach
London SW6 3JD
Tel: 020 7736 9520

De Pinna Notaries
35 Piccadilly
London W1J 0LJ
Tel: 020 7208 2900
Fax: 020 7208 0066
Email: info@depinna.co.uk
Website: www.depinna.co.uk

Fauchon Levy Khindria
Website: www.fauchonlevy.com

London office:

40 Doughty Street
London WC1N 2LF
Tel: 020 7430 0533
Fax: 020 7430 0540
Email: monique.fauchon@fauchonlevy.com

Paris office:

18 Avenue de la Bourdonnais
75007 Paris
Tel: 00 33 1 4753 0880
Fax: 00 33 1 4551 3416
Email: fauchon-levy@wanadoo.fr

John Howell & Co
The Old Glass Works
22 Endell Street
London WC2H 9AD
Tel: 020 7420 0400
Fax: 020 7836 3626

Appendix

Email: info@europelaw.com
Website: www.europelaw.com

Law Society
Tel: 020 7242 1222
Website: www.lawsociety.org.uk

The Law Society will have the details of solicitors who will be able to advise on French property.

Royal Institution of Chartered Surveyors
Surveyor Court
Westwood Way
Coventry CV4 8JE
Tel: 0870 333 1600
Fax: 020 7334 3811
Email: contactrics@rics.org
Website: www.rics.org.uk

It has the details of links with professionals who can survey properties around the world.

Letting property

Chez Nous
Spring Mill
Earby
Barnoldswick
Lancashire BB94 0AA
Tel: 0870 197 1000
Website: www.cheznous.com

French Country Cottages
Spring Mill
Earby
Barnoldswick
Lancashire BB94 0AA
Email: frenchcountrycottagespno@cendantvrg.co.uk
Tel: 0870 078 1500 (from UK)
Tel: 00 44 1282 846 144 (from overseas)
Website: www.french-country-cottages.co.uk

Buying Property in France

Holiday Rentals France
Tel: 020 8740 3865
Email: ross@holiday-rentals.com
Website: www.holiday-rentals.com

Newspapers/magazines

Bonjour Magazine
40 rue du 26 mars
24600, Ribérac
Tel: 00 33 5 5390 5495
Fax: 00 33 5 5390 5495
Email: fr@riberac.com
Website: www.bonjourmagazine.com

France Magazine
Freepost NAT17233 (for subscriptions only)
Market Harborough LE16 9BR
Tel: 01858 438 832
Fax: 01858 469 804
Website: www.francemag.com

French Property News
6 Burgess Mews
Wimbledon
London SW19 1UF
Website: www.french-property-news.com

Property France and Focus on France
Outbound Publishing
1 Commercial Road
Eastbourne
East Sussex BN21 3XQ
Tel: 01323 726 040
Website: www.outboundpublishing.com

Property organisations

L'Agence Nationale pour l'Amélioration de l'Habitat
Website: www.anah.fr

Appendix

Fédération Nationale des Agents Immobiliers et Mandataires (FNAIM)
Website: www.fnaim.fr

The leading association of estate agents in France.

Federation of Overseas Property Developers, Agents and Consultants
1st Floor
618 Newmarket Road
Cambridge CB5 8LP
Tel: 0870 350 1223
Fax: 0870 350 1233
Email: enquiries@fopdac.com
Website: www.fopdac.com

Unites agents, developers and specialist consultants active in the international property markets to protect sellers and buyers of overseas properties. There are strict criteria set in the Federation's Code of Ethics.

Syndicate National des Professionals Immobiliers (SNPI)
Website: www.snpi.com

An estate agent association.

Removals

British Association of Removers (BAR) Overseas
3 Churchill Court
58 Station Road
North Harrow HA2 7SA
Tel: 020 8861 3331
Fax: 020 8861 3332
Email: info@bar.co.uk
Website: www.barmovers.com

It has a section dealing with moving overseas.

Buying Property in France

General

Do not forget the Yellow Pages (*Pages Jaunes*) and google.com searches for agents and other useful information on France and its various regions.

Index

accessibility vii, xi, 60-1
    prices and 8
    travelling times 7-8, 9
agricultural properties 9, 35
air travel, on accessibility vii, xi, 7-8
animals 52-3

budgeting, on building 36
builders 33, 59
    fees 37
    insurance 34, 35
    restrictions 36, 61
    surveys from 27
building 31
    budgeting 36
    on exteriors 34-5
    insurance 34, 35
    payment 37
    preliminary checks 37
    restrictions 35, 58
    scope 33
    specific works 34
    see also new properties; off-plan properties; planning permission; renovation
business plans 43
businesses ix
    advice on 39
    finance options 43
    hotels and guest houses as 42
    investments as 39-40

    lettings as 40
    regulation 43
    restrictions 39, 43-4
    scope 39
    security in 43
    separate from homes 43
    see also property markets

Cannes 2, 3, 6
Capital Gains Tax 26, 55-6
Champagne-Ardenne 59-62
children, on inheritance 17-18
cities viii, 8, 57-8, 59
clear title 13
co-ownership 30
communes 2
completion 15, 16
condition of properties xi
condominium agreements 16-17
congeniality ix-x, 33, 51, 61-2
contracts
    builders 36
    on lettings 41
    option contracts 15
    planning permission in 34
    as preliminary ix, 13-14, 17, 24
conveyancing lawyers ix
    advice from 13
    fees 13, 24
    remit 12-13, 14, 15
Corporation Tax 19
costs 26
    grants on 25
    of selling properties 55
    see also fees; tax
culture ix-x, 3, 61-2
    scope 51
currency fluctuations 22-3

Index

deeds 15
departments 2
deposits 14, 15
developers 16
doctors, fees 52
drought 7

education
    enrolment 47
    scope 47-8
emigration *see* residence
employers 54, 61
employment 47
    dismissal 54
    scope 53-4
employment markets 47
estate agents 55, 60
    surveys from 28
EU citizenship 45-6
exteriors, building on 34-5

families 58, 60-1
fees 58
    builders 37
    doctors 52
    lawyers 13, 24-5
finance options 21, 43 *see also individual terms*
finding lawyers 12
finding properties 58, 60
    accessibility on 7-8, 9
    culture on 3
    deciding factors 1, 8
    hazards on 6-7
    location 1
    research x, 6, 7, 8-9, 10
    rural properties 9-10
    unknown factors 6
flooding 6-7

furnished lettings 42

government, local 1-2
grants, on costs 25
guarantees 16, 29
guest houses 42

hazards 6-7, 30
healthcare 52
historic monuments 35-6
holiday properties ix-x, 6, 11
hotels 42
hotspots 3

identity records 14
    for pets 53
immigration *see* residence
income, currency fluctuations on 22
Income Tax 54
inheritance ix, 17-18, 19
Inheritance Tax 18, 19
insurance
    for building 34, 35
    selling properties and 55
internet 8-9
investments 3, 6, 39-40

land, prices 5
language x
    learning 7
    scope 51-2
law vii, ix, xi-xii, 31
    scope 11
    see also individual terms
Law Society 12
lawyers
    conveyancing ix, 12-13, 14, 15, 24
    fees 24-5

Index

    hiring two 11-12
    from recommendation 12
    specialist 13
    time restrictions 11
leaseback schemes 17
lenders 23
lettings 8, 57-8
    furnished 42
    regulation 40
    restrictions 40
    safeguards 41
    scope 40
    tax and 41-2
    unfurnished 41-2
loans x
    currency fluctuations 22-3
    low-interest 25
    restrictions 22, 23
    see also mortgages
local government 1-2
location x-xi
    deciding factors 1
    exemptions viii
    prices and 1

management companies 17
matrimonial agreements 18
mayors 2
mortgage offers 24
mortgages x, 59
    currency fluctuations 22
    restrictions 23-4
    scope 22
    see also loans
municipalities 2

new properties xi
    guarantees 29

prices 4-5
scope 29
see also building; off-plan properties; planning permission
Nice 8
Normandy 6, 9-10

off-plan properties xi, 29
building on 16
commitment 15
completion 16
guarantees 16
safeguards 15, 16
warranties 16
see also building; new properties; planning permission
old properties
prices 4-5
renovation xi, 9, 10, 29, 33, 58, 59, 60, 61 *see also* building
option contracts 15
outline planning permission 34-5
outside agencies viii
ownership 15, 16
ascertaining 28-9
co-ownership 30
companies for 18-19
inheritance on 17-18, 19

parents, on inheritance 17-18
Paris 57-8, 59
passports, for pets 53
payment, for building 37
pets 52-3
planning permission 30-1
on agricultural properties 35
exemptions 34
historic monuments on 35-6
for hotels and guest houses 42
outline planning permission 34-5
preliminary checks 34

Index

    restrictions 35, 36
    scope 33
    see also building; new properties; off-plan properties; renovation
popularity vii-viii
precautions 3, 6, 10, 29, 41, 59 *see also individual terms*
preliminary contracts ix, 24
    commitment in 13-14
    cooling-off periods 14
    deposits in 14
    identity records for 14
    on ownership 17
    scope 14
prices 3, 6, 59
    accessibility and 8
    location and 1
    rising viii
    scope 4-5
property markets viii
    disparities x
    hotspots 3
    investments 3, 6, 39-40
    see also businesses

quality of life 61-2
quotes, for building 36

rail travel, on accessibility 7-8
real-life stories 57 *see also individual terms*
receipts, for building 37
regions 2
renovation xi, 9, 10, 29, 59, 60, 61
    restrictions 58
    sympathetic 33
    see also building; planning permission
rent 3, 6, 40
    rent based tax 25-6
renting xi, 45

Buying Property in France

residence ix-x, 59-62
    education in 47-8
    employment in 47
    EU citizenship and 45-6
    preliminary checks 45
    regulation 45-6
    renting before 45
    restrictions 46
    on retirement 46
    time restrictions 46
resorts 2, 3, 6, 8, 11
retirement 46
retreats 6, 9-10, 59-62
rural properties 6, 9-10, 11, 35, 59-62

Schengen Agreement 46
searches 15, 31
self-employment 58
    VAT 54-5
selling properties
    Capital Gains Tax 55-6
    costs 55
    insurance and 55
    scope 55
    VAT 56
service charges 30
sewers 30
skiing properties 11
spouses, on inheritance 18, 19
surveyors
    restrictions 27-8
    scope 27, 28
surveys 31
    from builders 27
    from estate agents 28
    scope 28

tax 24

Index

    Capital Gains Tax 26, 55-6
    on company ownership 18-19
    Corporation Tax 19
    on costs 25
    Income Tax 54
    Inheritance Tax 18, 19
    lettings and 41-2
    on occupiers 25
    rent based 25-6
    VAT 54-5, 56
    wealth based 26
tenants 41
timeshares 16
title, clear 13
town halls 34-5
transfers of money 15, 16
travelling times 7-8, 9

unfurnished lettings 41-2
utilities 31
    water 30

valuations 28
VAT 54-5, 56

warranties 16
water mains 30
wealth based tax 26
Wills 19

89

Notes

Notes

Notes

Notes

Notes

Notes

Notes

Notes